Self-Love

SELF-LOVE

100+ QUOTES, REFLECTIONS, and ACTIVITIES
to HELP YOU UNCOVER and STRENGTHEN
Your Self-Love

Devi B. Dillard-Wright

ADAMS MEDIA
New York London Toronto Sydney New Delhi

Adams Media
An Imprint of Simon & Schuster, Inc.
57 Littlefield Street
Avon, Massachusetts 02322

First Adams Media hardcover edition January 2021

ADAMS MEDIA and colophon are trademarks of Simon & Schuster.

For information about special discounts for bulk purchases, please contact Simon & Schuster Special Sales at 1-866-506-1949 or business@simonandschuster.com.

The Simon & Schuster Speakers Bureau can bring authors to your live event. For more information or to book an event contact the Simon & Schuster Speakers Bureau at 1-866-248-3049 or visit our website at www.simonspeakers.com.

Interior design and illustrations by Priscilla Yuen

Manufactured in China

10 9 8 7 6 5 4 3 2 1

Library of Congress Cataloging-in-Publication Data
Names: Dillard-Wright, Devi B., author.
Title: Self-love / Devi B. Dillard-Wright.
Description: Avon, Massachusetts: Adams Media, 2021.
Identifiers: LCCN 2020035001 | ISBN 9781507214299 (hc) | ISBN 9781507214305 (ebook)
Subjects: LCSH: Self-acceptance--Quotations, maxims, etc. | Conduct of life--Quotations, maxims, etc.
Classification: LCC BF575.S37 D545 2021 | DDC 158.1--dc23
LC record available at https://lccn.loc.gov/2020035001

ISBN 978-1-5072-1429-9
ISBN 978-1-5072-1430-5 (ebook)

Dedicated to the Black Lives Matter movement.

Special thanks to Eileen Mullan, Sarah Doughty, and the whole team at Adams Media for making this book happen. Thanks to my partner, Jess, and to my kids, Atticus, Oscar, and Tallulah.

Contents

Introduction

You may have heard the term "self-love" before, perhaps in the context of body image or pampering activities, but what does it truly mean to have self-love? At its core, self-love is an unconditional acceptance of and value for yourself—body, mind, and soul. Confidence in your decisions, appreciation for your strengths *and* weaknesses, and care for your physical and mental needs are all part of loving yourself.

Self-love is not something that shows up one day as an unchanging, constant companion through life, however. It is not something you are born with or without. Self-love is a journey, full of twists and turns, each day an opportunity to move one step forward through loving intention and practice. Of course, it can be difficult to know where to start: As a transgender person and published teacher in the healing practices of mindfulness and meditation, I understand there is so much that goes into loving yourself, from past experiences to the influences and relationships that surround us. So, how do you begin to weed through your own history and personal challenges to cultivate self-love? This book is here to help.

Self-Love offers over one hundred lessons, reflections, quotes, and activities to help you manifest and nurture true love for yourself. Gathered from numerous well-established disciplines, including the Hindu and Buddhist traditions, as well as my own background that includes decades of professional experience regarding self-worth, the insights you will discover here are not single-purpose solutions intended to ease just one moment of self-doubt. You will go directly to the root of the problem, looking at the ways you think about and speak to yourself. By targeting the underlying obstacles that weigh on your self-esteem, you will heal past wounds and rewire the harmful behaviors that have kept you from self-love.

But, before you dive into the lessons and practices in this book, take some time to look through the opening part on the principles of self-love. Here you will explore what it means to have self-love and why it is a crucial part of a fulfilling life. Think of this as your own first step toward loving yourself. With it, you will be able to make the most of each insight and activity that follows. Your journey to a more confident, happier you begins now!

Part 1
UNDERSTANDING SELF-LOVE

Every day, you participate in the human condition, which carries with it a great deal of uncertainty about who you are and your place in the world. From an unexpected obstacle at work to difficulties within a friendship, opportunities for self-doubt and a diminished sense of your worth exist around every corner, but opportunities for self-love also exist at each of these turns. You can choose to fall to criticism and strife, or you can journey toward greater confidence and appreciation for the unique person you are. You can love yourself at your best and also love yourself when you are feeling less than wonderful. Self-love operates in all these changing circumstances; it is the anchor that allows you to weather life's ups and downs and thrive in the best *and* worst conditions.

In this part, you will dive deeper into what it means to have self-love and why practicing self-love is so important. From resilience in the face of life's challenges to stronger relationships with those around you, self-love is a key to unlocking your potential and expanding your world. Of course, for many, self-love can feel difficult, which is why this part explores methods for cultivating and maintaining love for yourself no matter where life takes you.

What Is Self-Love?

When you think about self-love, certain themes may come to mind, like accepting your body as it is or speaking to yourself kindly when life gets challenging. Maybe you think of self-care—loving activities to do for yourself to help clear out negative thoughts or feelings and recharge. Each of these is a part of self-love. Body acceptance, self-compassion, and intentional care for your physical and emotional health are all smaller pieces that make up how you see and feel about yourself. When you love yourself, you place your happiness in the highest regard. You value your thoughts and feelings and have confidence in your abilities. You accept and appreciate who you are, inside and out.

Why Should I Practice Self-Love?

You can find shelves and shelves of advice about solving this or that problem (making money, losing weight, finding a partner), but these pursuits fall short when you don't have love for who you are as a person. Money, weight loss, and romance can help you feel good in the moment, but life is always in motion, and each of these factors can change from one instant to the next. The only thing you can be sure you will always have is yourself, so why not love who you are?

For many, a big part of the focus on making more money, losing a few pounds, or finding a partner is validation from others. Maybe you want to be recognized in your career and move up the ranks, or you want to make more money so you can purchase things that look nice and will be complimented by other people. It feels good to receive praise, and there's nothing wrong with that! We are social beings, after all; it's natural to want other people to think well of us. The problem comes when you are unable to rely on internal validation in the moments when those external compliments and rewards aren't present. There may be days when a work project flops, a favorite pair of pants is a little snug, or you don't have any spending money. In these moments, you will need a strong and dependable source of positivity and confidence in your life that will always be with you, no matter what is happening in your life. Self-love can be that powerful source. Feeling unconvinced? Just as there is no one quality that defines self-love, there is also no one benefit to loving yourself. A sense of self-love extends into every part of your life, from your ability to bounce back from unexpected challenges to your connections with those around you. We will explore the benefits of self-love more in the following sections.

Resilience

In 2011, University of Arizona psychologist David A. Sbarra studied a group of over one hundred people going through a divorce. Participants were scored using a standardized measure of several factors, including self-kindness (an important part of self-love that means treating yourself with understanding and forgiveness). The study found that those who scored higher in self-kindness tended to exhibit less emotional disturbance and adjusted better to the divorce. This is not to say they didn't feel any pain from the experience, but they were better at not blaming themselves for things going wrong and did not get stuck in negative emotions as frequently as participants who scored lower in self-kindness. Sbarra also concluded that self-kindness is teachable and that teaching self-kindness could become an effective treatment for people going through a divorce.

Self-love also builds resilience in the day-to-day struggles we each face. In a collection of five different studies, Duke University psychologist Mark R. Leary found that people who scored highly in self-compassion tended to react less negatively to small stressors in everyday life, and that this same self-compassion had a "buffering" effect when imagining potential stressful social situations. These participants were able to accept their own contributions to negative events (procrastinating on a deadline, spending too much on dinner) without underestimating their ability to overcome these problems. Self-love provided a point of balance between the extremes of arrogance and self-deprecation.

Personal Growth

Self-love can help you navigate challenges, but can treating yourself kindly after a mistake lead to increased motivation to improve on the area or areas where this mistake may have originated? Juliana Breines (most recently of the University of Rhode Island) and Serena Chen of the University of California, Berkeley, wanted to answer this question. In a series of experiments designed to test how people feel about personal failings, as well as lackluster academic performance, Breines and Chen found that people who had self-love recognized their failings but were also motivated to improve upon their past performance. As Breines and Chen wrote, "[s]elf-compassion...provides a safe and nonjudgmental context to confront negative aspects of the self and strive to better them."

Emotional Release

Research also shows that self-love can help you let go of harmful feelings such as anger and hurt. A study conducted at Moa Oasis in Israel asked participants suffering from clinical levels of anger to record loving messages to themselves in their own voices. They then played these messages back to themselves for two minutes every day over a period of twelve weeks. By the end of the twelve-week period, researchers observed a significant decrease in negative feelings, suggesting that self-love can be effective in reducing afflictive emotions.

Stronger Relationships

Self-love plays an important role in all your relationships, not just the one you have with yourself. Lacking self-love can mean lower expectations of your relationships and those close to you. You may overlook harmful behaviors in a romantic partner or friend, for example, or even consider that you might not deserve any better. You may also find it difficult to stick up for yourself in a relationship as self-doubt overshadows any confidence in your own opinions. When you have self-love, you seek healthy relationships that lift you up and you walk away from those that pull you down. You are also comfortable with being alone instead of looking to others for your own happiness or sense of security.

Why Does It Feel Difficult to Love Myself?

You may be thinking that self-love doesn't come easily for you. Maybe self-criticisms sneak in whenever things feel challenging or doubting yourself seems like a natural part of the decisions you make throughout each day. These unkind thoughts have likely become automatic over time, and, like any established habit, their roots require intentional, regular effort to dig up so you can sow self-love in their place.

Of course, the challenges in self-love don't just come from within. In today's world of ever-advancing technology, you have more information accessible to you than ever before. In many ways it's a blessing, helping you answer questions at the push of a button and keeping you in touch with friends and family, but it can also be a negative influence on your sense of self-worth. From advertisements promising younger skin and rapid weight loss to the carefully curated highlight reels on *Instagram*, it's easy to fall into the comparison trap, measuring yourself against the perfectly edited photos of others and their exciting (or at least *seemingly* exciting) lives. The truth is that self-love is a journey: You don't simply flip a switch and suddenly love and accept everything about yourself. Just as self-doubt and negative self-talk were cultivated over time and experience, it will take practice to rewire these habits into self-confidence and compassion toward yourself.

As you begin practicing self-love in the lessons throughout this book, it may feel strange at first—to speak positively about yourself, to look in the mirror and express love for what you see—but as you continue your journey with intention, self-love will eventually come more naturally. If ever you feel yourself losing motivation, remember that there are tried-and-true methods for self-love, methods around which the lessons in this book are built. The following sections will provide an overview of these methods. You are now on your way to a more confident, self-compassionate you!

How Do I Practice Self-Love?

The journey toward self-love involves effort on several different fronts: your mental state, your body, your connections with others, and your professional life. We will explore each of these elements of self-love, as well as general practices for nurturing them. The activities found in the lessons of Part 2 draw on these practices.

Self-Love and Your Mind

One of the most important parts of your journey revolves around your mental state. This is where self-doubt and unkind thoughts toward yourself are born. Practices in self-love replace this negative, judgmental thinking with positive, encouraging thoughts about yourself. Meditation is a great tool for clearing the mind of negativity and manifesting the mental state you desire. I recommend a regular meditation practice of at least twenty minutes a day. Simply acknowledging hurtful self-talk is also an easy place to start as these thoughts are often so immediate and automatic that you may not even realize how frequent and unkind they are until you begin to intentionally notice each one. Consider seeing a therapist for mental health issues as well. It's important to reach out to others when you need a little help.

Self-Love and Your Body

Self-love also means taking care of your physical body and what is known as your "embodied mind." This refers to the idea that the mind and the body are not opposed to one another but are part of one reality, feeding into one another. Good mental habits lead to good physical habits and vice versa. Caring for your embodied mind is an important way of showing love and respect for yourself. Over time, these acts of self-love will become more natural.

You can start nurturing self-love through physical care with easy, commonsense steps like getting physical exercise every day, cutting back on junk food, eating fresh fruits and vegetables, going to the doctor when you're sick or injured, and keeping up with wellness visits.

To manifest self-love through the embodied mind, you will need to pay attention to your physical surroundings and be careful about your exposure to harmful influences. Advertising can be a powerful trigger for low self-esteem, so try spending less time browsing media that fosters unrealistic expectations, such as impossible beauty standards or displays of wealth. You might think about installing an ad blocker on your web browser as well and reading books instead of magazines.

Low self-esteem can also point to some form of deprivation in your life. You may take care of others to the detriment of your own health, for example. Treat yourself in a sustainable way by making a spending plan that includes special items for yourself. These could be anything from yoga classes to a regular manicure to a new outfit that amps up your confidence.

Self-Love and Your Working Life

A more overlooked aspect of self-love is your relationship with your work. A job that's mindless can cultivate feelings of low self-worth as you aren't working toward something you feel proud of. However, a job that is overly taxing can make you feel underappreciated. Eventually, believing that others don't value you can lead to questions of whether your skills and time are actually worth appreciating.

Now is a good time to evaluate your attitude toward work. Think about what drew you to your career in the first place. Concentrate on the aspects of the job you love the most and channel your energies in that direction. If you've been in the same position for awhile, it may be time to consider professional development. Attend a training that will break open a new area of interest for you, either within the job you have or within a job you might want to pursue. To avoid feeling undervalued, ensure you are working reasonable hours and that the tasks you take on fall under your job description. If you can't, it may be time to talk to your employer about a raise or promotion.

Work-Life Balance

Nurturing self-love in your professional life also means ensuring balance between work and your personal life. It's hard to be happy if you are overworked and overtired, neglecting the personal hobbies and relationships that fill your emotional reserves. On the other hand, too much focus on your personal life makes it difficult to work effectively within a professional role and can be a detriment to the career aspirations that would have helped you feel fulfilled and empowered. Finding a balance that allows you to thrive in both aspects of your life cultivates a happiness that influences your view of the world and how you feel about yourself. At home, drawing a concrete line between work and personal hours can be one of the easiest ways to keep this balance and reconnect with your partner or family members. Try playing board games or doing puzzles together and sitting down collectively for dinner at least a few nights a week.

What Now?

You are taking the first steps toward a happier, more fulfilling life, inside and out, and that's something to be proud of! As you work through the lessons and activities in this book, keep two things in mind. First, this is a day-by-day journey. Each day brings new opportunities and challenges, and taking small steps regularly will help you navigate your journey to self-love without becoming overwhelmed. Second, this is also a long-term journey. There will likely be ups and downs as you practice loving yourself and explore the thoughts and feelings that have weighed on your self-esteem over the years, but you will also be building a foundation of self-love that can carry you through these ebbs and flows.

The Self-Love Pledge

To provide additional help on your journey, the following is a special pledge you can say each day to remind yourself of your dedication to discovering all the wonderful things that make you worth loving. Use it as a template and alter as needed to fit your personal goals in self-love:

> *Each day I commit myself to loving and respecting who I am. I care for myself—mentally, spiritually, and physically—so I can be present in my life and with everyone in it. I dedicate myself to finding and exploring my own nature and expressing myself in the world. I recognize that my personal good intersects with the good all around me. In thinking, acting, and feeling, I align all my priorities with my personal growth.*

Consider writing this pledge on a separate piece of paper and storing it in this book or posting it in your home in a place where you'll see it regularly, such as the bathroom mirror. Begin and end each day by reciting it.

Getting Started

Now that you've explored the ins and outs of self-love and what makes it so important to a happy, fulfilling life, it's time to dive into the lessons, reflections, quotes, and activities that will help you cultivate and maintain self-love through whatever life throws your way. Devote yourself to reading the following pages with an open mind and an open heart: You deserve the effort! It's time to love yourself for the unique person you are, both inside and out.

Part 2

PRACTICING SELF-LOVE

You have reflected on what it really means to love yourself and how it applies to the different parts of your life. You have seen how your inner feelings about yourself affect your health and success, and how you respond to the unexpected. Of course, understanding what it means to have self-love and why it is important is just the beginning of your journey. It will take practice to break down your own barriers in loving yourself and truly accept and appreciate who you are.

This part includes over one hundred lessons, reflections, activities, and inspirational quotes to help you banish self-doubt and recognize all the wonderful, unique things that make you worth loving. Since some activities involve reflective writing, it might be a good idea to keep a designated notebook for these exercises, as well as to jot down any additional insights you have. Have fun with these exercises and personalize them however you like. Underline things that stand out to you most, bookmark activities and lessons you want to return to later or share with someone else, and remember that, as in any journey, the experiences and growth you manifest in self-love come down to the effort you put in. You are worth each and every step forward!

If you celebrate your differentness, the world will too. It believes exactly what you tell it—through the words you use to describe yourself, the actions you take to care for yourself, and the choices you make to express yourself. Tell the world you are a one-of-a-kind creation who came here to experience wonder and spread joy. Expect to be accommodated.

—Victoria Moran, author of *Lit from Within: Tending Your Soul for Lifelong Beauty*

Loving yourself isn't vanity.
It's sanity.

—André Gide, Nobel Prize–winning author

Choose the Best Role for You

In reality, not a single one of us is so magically normative as to claim the right to separate out the freaks from everyone else. We are all freaks to someone. Maybe even—if we're honest—to ourselves....For that matter, if we're all someone's "freak," does this mean that we are all each other's "normal" too—and worthy of embrace?

—Gwendolyn Ann Smith, author of "We're All Someone's Freak," part of *Gender Outlaws: The Next Generation*

Sometimes you can put yourself through so much grief trying to be what you think other people want you to be. You try to fit into the roles mapped out for you by society: the strong man, the loving wife, the good child. In some instances, there are responsibilities within these expectations that do benefit your life and the lives of those you care about. For example, acting the part of a professional in the workplace can help you land a promotion, and continue being successful in your career. However, a larger part of these pressures from the outside world simply makes you forget to ask what it is *you* want. Through ignoring your own desires, you are expressing that what you want isn't worth considering. It is a sneaky form of self-doubt that weighs on your appreciation for who you are and what you have to offer. You may not be able to silence the voices of those social expectations, but you can choose the role that feels best to you. Remember: Despite what others might lead you to believe, *you* are the lead in your own life. Each day there are new opportunities for choices that nurture the role in which you feel truly happy. Unsure of what that role is just yet? The choices you make to follow what feels right in the moment can help you figure it out.

TAKING ACTION

Think about the ways you censor yourself to please others. Maybe you hold back from speaking in conversations or wear clothes that don't really please you. See if you can change the way you play your part so you find more satisfaction in your life. Do one small thing today to get out of line with your typical behavior. It doesn't have to be anything huge: Wear a top you might otherwise leave in the back of the closet or simply say hello to someone new.

Embrace the Uncomfortable

You are beautiful because of your unrelenting insistence on being utterly, uncompromisingly, completely you.

—Jeanette LeBlanc, writer

In order to get to the place of your dreams, a place where you accept and love yourself, you first have to set aside the comfortable ways that you have known. Moving into a place of self-love requires a certain amount of discomfort. You are trying something new—truly loving and accepting yourself—and with that comes uncertainty. After all, nothing is static. The world and every life in it changes with each passing day. Movement toward the unknown can be difficult because you have to relinquish control over what may happen, and you may even be confronted by hidden aspects of yourself that you have previously been afraid to bring into the light. This hidden self might be the poet who wants to find readers, the queer person who wants to come out of the closet, or the musician who wants to play for an audience. Each one of us contains many different worlds and perspectives. The process of cultivating self-love involves viewing reality through a different lens and embracing all aspects of who you are. This process can be difficult, but it carries rewards that would be unknown without the struggle of growing. Growing as a person does not have to mean perfectionism or competition. It can just mean taking a dormant part of yourself and giving it expression. Your self-expression does not have to be *Instagram*-perfect, either. It can be something small that only you can see.

TAKING ACTION

Is there some hidden aspect of yourself that makes you a little uncomfortable? Take a small step today to let it out in the open. Go and visit an art gallery, pick up a book of poetry, or do anything that speaks to your inner weirdness. Give yourself a little bit of time and space today that nurtures your inner self.

Create Balance

Optimal self-esteem is grounded in reality
in that the individual has adopted a balanced
perspective on his/her strengths and weaknesses,
including the search for learning opportunities that
will further self-understanding and
avoid future failures.

—Susan Harter, author of *The Construction of the Self:*
Developmental and Sociocultural Foundations, second edition

Self-love has an internal paradox: If you become overly involved with yourself, you fall into the bad kind of narcissism that disconnects you from the world and strains your relationships as you are unable to think of anyone else's needs or desires. But if you become too self-effacing, you lose your sense of self entirely, which can lead to resentful or begrudging service of others at the expense of your well-being. Your focus is so fixed on other people that you may not even notice your own accomplishments and skills, your own wonderful qualities. The point of balance can feel elusive, but it lies in a flexible kind of negotiation with the world around you, in a practice of give and take that meets your needs and the needs of those you care about.

TAKING ACTION

See if you can spot these extremes in your own life: times when you had an inflated sense of self and times when you thought little of yourself. An example of an inflated sense of self might be taking pride in something that is the bare minimum, like showing up for work. An example of thinking too little of yourself might be saying, "I always mess things up," or "I'll never be able to get a date." What might a balance between extremes look like for you at this point in your journey?

Rethink Your Idols

The cult of celebrity, in essence, is a distraction from our own progression as human beings....Of course, an indulgent look every now and then is part of humanity, but perhaps if we were to stop looking for hope in false gods and focus more on our own talents and unique identities we'd waste far less time trying to be like someone else.

—Greg French, fashion writer

As a member of the species that sociologist Mircea Eliade coined *homo religiosus*, you are a meaning-making creature. You seek out associations between objects and events and are drawn by human instinct to desire deeper significance within them. And there is nothing wrong with that… until the symbols you choose for yourself become too limiting or even destructive. Too often, celebrities are placed on a pedestal where any shortcomings, no matter how great, are ignored or excused outright. When a person is held up as a god, no one wants to see their faults. You may sometimes idolize deeply flawed and even abusive people, or choose a role model who may be too far out of reach, like an airbrushed supermodel. This focus on the unobtainable, revering something that may not even exist, only leads to disparaging yourself as you are. Meanwhile, the real thing—a genuinely kind, intelligent, or courageous person—may already be in your life. By recognizing good qualities like generosity, patience, and creativity in those around you, you choose role models who motivate you each day to be your own best self and to love the good qualities within yourself.

TAKING ACTION

Look back over your life so far. Did a chosen ideal or model of life ever become too limiting? Has a role model ever let you down or tried to take advantage of you? Who are your idols now? Who or what do you worship and how do these idols affect your sense of self-love?

Live More, Conquer Less

Living as love changed me in every way. In the past, I tried to make things happen and force results, but that has morphed into accepting life on its terms, which has given me a peace beyond understanding. I started to see joy and sorrow as two sides of the same coin. No longer bound by the pain of resistance, I welcomed changes as they came to me, seeing everything as part of a cosmic whole.

—Marj Britt, Unity minister

Too often we look at life as trying to get somewhere, to be more "successful." This questing or conquering view of life has its place—you can find a lot of motivation in a worthy goal—but the motivational worldview can also rob ordinary moments of their beauty and liveliness, and it keeps us from loving what is. You don't have to be conquering all the time to have a happy, fulfilling life. You can live and love right where you are. This moment matters, just as it is. You matter. You can afford to stop and reflect. You can take stock of the day: what you've done and left undone. You can take time to give thanks, to rest, to just be. You are not a whole person worthy of loving yourself just when you are accomplishing things. You are actually *most* human in your moments of weakness, when you don't have it all together. You can love yourself right now, just as you are. You deserve it.

TAKING ACTION
Take a moment now to just be. Let go of the tendency to hurry and accomplish. Let go of the aggression that would have you conquer the day. Simply rest for a few minutes to enjoy what is and who you are right now. The world will be there for you when you're ready.

Forgive Someone

Until we can forgive,
we remain locked in our pain and
locked out of the possibility of
experiencing healing and freedom,
locked out of the possibility
of being at peace.

—Archbishop Desmond Tutu,
recipient of the Nobel Peace Prize

The love of oneself and the love of others are deeply entwined. These loves depend upon one another and flow into each other. If you do not accept the person next to you, you will carry anger and resentment. These heavy emotions, if left unchecked, will eventually lead to a harmful relationship with yourself as you seek to purge them through destructive behaviors such as lashing out or withdrawing from other relationships. If you can recognize in your fellow human being a flawed but intrinsically valuable person, you will be able to forgive them for their mistakes and imperfections. And don't think of forgiveness as something that only operates in the past tense, as in forgiving past wrongs, but as something that operates in the present, an openness to a real encounter. All real encounters take place with imperfect beings, just like you.

TAKING ACTION

Make a list of the people who have hurt you or let you down in ways you are still holding on to. Now go down this list and envision yourself forgiving at least one of these people. You can even say "I forgive you" out loud to help solidify the experience or reach out to that person to forgive them in person. Forgiveness does not mean you have to forget what happened or say that you are okay with what that person did; it can simply mean a readiness to be released from the past.

Allow Yourself to Mourn

Grief is a full-body experience. It takes over your entire body—it's not a disease of the mind....There are certain things that happen to you as a human being that you cannot control or command, that will come to you at really inconvenient times, and where you have to bow in the human humility to the fact that there's something running through you that's bigger than you.

—Elizabeth Gilbert, author

You mourn for those who have died, but you also mourn for those who still live. You make connections and sometimes lose them later in life. Relationships bend and break, sometimes permanently. You can also grieve for lost places or times gone by. These experiences and feelings of loss become part of you—of how you view the world, choose future relationships, and deal with the changes of life. These losses are not to be excised, anesthetized, or suppressed. Keep returning to the touchstones of loss in your own life to find reminders of who you were and who you want to be moving forward. The pain and sweetness of life intertwine. Loss is a part of loving yourself. To love is to risk losing, but any loss you might experience holds lessons, as well as the potential for even more happiness and love in place of what has ended.

TAKING ACTION

Take a few minutes to go back to a time when you deeply mourned a loss in your life. Maybe you remember the loss of a parent or grandparent, a treasured place like a childhood home, or a beloved pet. Write about your experience: What happened? How did that loss help make you the person you are today? What are you proud of in the way you've dealt with or overcome your pain?

Grow Up, Don't Give Up

Many of us were taught as children that we shouldn't express ourselves too much. We should pipe down in some way. Such children often become adults who are in the habit of cowering, as though we're afraid of taking up too much space. Our mind then comes into conflict with our soul's knowing. Because each of us is the center of the universe, we are here to express ourselves, and on some level we know this.

—Marianne Williamson, author of *The Law of Divine Compensation: On Work, Money, and Miracles*

At some point in your life, you may have decided to present to the world a kind of toned-down version of yourself, with all the rough places smoothed out and the wilder bits firmly tamped down. You try to reassure others that you're quite safe and ordinary, that you won't make waves. This change, usually labeled as growing up or maturing, has a downside, as you can end up losing something of the spark that is your unique contribution to the world. Somehow you have to learn to grow up without giving up the sense of uniqueness and wonder that is inherent in childhood. If you've already let go of this quirkiness or set aside that open curiosity along the path to adulthood, it's time to reclaim it. Being yourself and loving yourself are two sides of the same coin, two ways to reach greater fulfillment and joy. Self-love unfolds through the practices that allow your true self to shine.

TAKING ACTION

Have you lost some of that unique spark in your own life? Rediscover what is special about you by doing one thing today that will help you get in touch with your inner child. Try drawing a picture or playing outside. Set a timer and give your pursuit at least fifteen minutes.

Listen to Your Body

We must not minimize or negate the impact of being told to hate or fear our bodies and the bodies of others. Living in a society structured to profit from our self-hate creates a dynamic in which we are so terrified of being ourselves that we adopt terror-based ways of being in our bodies. All this is fueled by a system that makes large quantities of money off our shame and bias.

—Sonya Renee Taylor, activist and author of *The Body Is Not an Apology: The Power of Radical Self-Love*

Self-love means loving all the parts of who you are, including the body that carries you from one day to the next. Of course, the body is an unruly creature: It resists your attempts to push it into predetermined molds, it escapes your plans for management and control, it holds injuries and scars, imbalances and brokenness, but it also holds messages for how to care for it and how to nourish your unique needs. That knot in your shoulders calls for yoga and massage. The tension in your head asks for a respite from work. Your tired eyes beg to close. When you open yourself to the messages contained within your own body, you take control over not just your health but your happiness as well. A body is not just a body: It is a vehicle for expression, a cabinet of curiosities, a record of events, a palace of pleasure, and a storehouse of wisdom. By listening to its needs and supporting its desires, you can begin to access this inner reserve and recognize just how amazing and deserving of love your body is.

TAKING ACTION

Take a few minutes to do a body scan meditation, observing your body from the tips of your toes to the crown of your head. Look for the places where you might be holding on to pain and fatigue. Ask your body to show you how you can be kinder to it, how you can give it relief from the aches and pains of everyday life. Give yourself permission to follow the needs and inclinations of your physical self.

Be Present

We do not have to go anywhere in order to touch our true nature. The wave does not have to look for water because she is water. We do not have to look for God, we do not have to look for our ultimate dimension or nirvana, because we are nirvana, we are God. You are what you are looking for. You are already what you want to become.

—Thich Nhat Hanh, Buddhist monk and author of
No Death, No Fear: Comforting Wisdom for Life

People spend the vast amount of their time on Earth worrying about things they did in the past or trying to attain something in the future. Mindfulness meditation teaches something so simple that it shouldn't be a revelation but nonetheless never fails to surprise: The past and the future don't exist. You only have the present. The present holds so much beauty, and you may never even notice it because past regrets and future expectations lead you to flee from it so quickly. However, this present moment is the only place where self-love can take place. Awareness of the present moment helps you fully experience and appreciate the good things in your life and yourself. Of course, it can feel difficult to pay deep attention solely to what is occurring right now, which is why mindfulness practices such as meditation are so beneficial. Daily meditation helps keep your mind focused on the present.

TAKING ACTION

Take a few minutes to simply observe everything that is happening inside your head and in the room where you are reading this book. Take the role of an observer, noticing the tiniest details that enter your awareness. As thoughts about the past and future come into your mind, gently acknowledge and then let go of them. See if you can maintain this habit of quiet observation while going about your everyday activities.

Connect with Like-Minded People

A real love I'm searchin.'
A real love.
I found and I call them kin.
Kinfolk.

—Kai M. Green, black queer scholar

Think of the self as a switchboard, an old-timey telephone exchange. This exchange has all sorts of colorful lights that only illuminate when a particular call goes through—no connections means no lights. To illuminate yourself, you have to plug in, to connect, with others who share the same goals, interests, and inclinations, otherwise the switchboard will be dark, dull, and dreary. You have to connect with people who make you feel less alone in the world, who have the words you've been wanting to hear, people who "get it." Forming this community of like-minded people helps you improve your sense of appreciation and love for yourself as you give expression to the unique parts of your identity. If you can't find these people in real life, you can seek them out in virtual spaces. Sometimes virtual encounters turn into friendships beyond the keyboard. No matter how you go about it, you need to connect with others who understand and encourage the person you are.

TAKING ACTION

Think for a few minutes about the people in your life. What parts of yourself do they connect to and help you express? Think of a few ways to expand your network, including looking into joining organizations or clubs focused on your values or passions.

Indulge Your Curiosity

*A first step toward empathy might seem paradoxical:
we may have to discover our own worth and have a
basis for self-concern. It is impossible to appreciate
the complexity of others if we are not able to love
ourselves, knowing our contradictions. A positive
love for one's own soul then might extend beyond
oneself to include the world, and it might have more
weight than an abstract tolerance of humankind.*

—Thomas Moore, writer and poet

Manifesting greater self-love means getting curious about yourself—
exploring your own motivations, feelings, and thoughts. Why did you
react that way? What do you want right now? Why are you feeling this
way? This curiosity leads to compassion toward yourself as you better
understand where harmful thoughts, feelings, and behaviors stem from.
And as you practice inward curiosity along your journey to self-love, you

may also begin to practice more outward curiosity, wanting to know how other people live in the world and how their own journeys of self-love are unfolding. Curiosity becomes a pursuit that makes the world endlessly enthralling. You begin wanting to know things just for the sake of knowing, and that makes life all the more worthwhile. The compassion you develop for yourself also becomes a greater understanding toward other people.

TAKING ACTION

Think for a bit about your natural curiosity. What would you like to know? Maybe you'd like to learn Italian or to ride a bike or to make a giant playlist. Find one small thing that makes you curious right now and spend a few minutes investigating that nugget of curiosity.

Allow Room for Spontaneity

*There is something scary about letting ourselves go.
It means that we will screw up, that we will relinquish the
possibility of perfection. It means that we will say things we
didn't mean to say and express feelings we can't explain.
It means that we will be onstage and not have complete
control, that we won't know what we are going to play
until we begin, until the bow is drawn across the strings.*

—Jonah Lehrer, author of *Imagine: How Creativity Works*

It sounds like a funny thing to say, but you probably do not often improvise in your own life. You may practice conversations ahead of time in the shower, the shampoo and conditioner bottles acting as stand-ins for the people you will be talking to. Maybe your home is littered with to-do lists or outlines for each day. You may even have a plan drawn out for the next year—or five, or ten! These days, plotting your every move is easier than ever, thanks to the dozens of task management apps and electronic calendars and notes. Of course, planning ahead is by no means a bad thing. Keeping yourself organized helps you stay on track with your deadlines and goals. However, to be your unique self, you also need a bit of spontaneity in life. When everything is planned in advance, it can feel like you are more of a programmed robot than an actual living being. Allowing yourself room to improvise along the way is a simple act of self-love that encourages time for whatever makes you feel alive and thriving in the moment. By making space for spontaneity in your schedule, you are showing yourself that you are more than a producer: You are a being of flesh and blood and heart. You deserve a bit of excitement among all those to-dos.

TAKING ACTION

Think about how much planning and how much spontaneity you have in your life. Are these two ends of the spectrum balanced or wildly unequal? Do something today that is outside of your schedule, without regard for making money or optimizing efficiency.

Suspend Judgment

All judgment is,
in one way or another,
self-judgment.

—Joseph Rain, author of *The Unfinished Book about Who*
We Are: Book One: First Steps to Self-Discovery

As a human being, you pay a price for having consciousness: You can no longer perceive the world without the labels of objects and relationships, together with all of the cultural associations and inherited biases that come with those labels. This means you do not see yourself directly or objectively. Your perspective is clouded with all the labels that often question your worth and foster doubt in who you are. To truly accept and ultimately love yourself and your life as is, you have to suspend judgment, to refrain from, if only for an instant, the need to define your perceptions. This suspension of judgment is the true goal of meditation, and you can practice it anytime, anywhere, by temporarily letting go of the veil of language that separates you from sensual objects. To allow suspension of judgment, you must release certainty and replace it with an attitude of "maybe" or "it could be the case that…" See your thoughts as provisional and partial in nature, as obscuring reality rather than revealing it. Let loose those labels and welcome self-compassion in their place.

TAKING ACTION

To practice suspension of judgment, think of some of the labels you might apply to yourself; for example, "parent," "writer," "American," etc. As these thoughts come to you, don't negate them; simply see them without affirmation or denial. Recognize them as provisional truths that do not speak to your whole self. See the partiality of these labels.

Work Around Fear

Fear is only as deep as the mind allows.

—Japanese proverb

You may have some phobias or fears that hold you back in life. Maybe you're afraid of snakes, dogs, or clowns. You may be afraid to speak in public or have trouble interacting in large gatherings. Or perhaps you're afraid to get on an airplane or drive over bridges. Fears don't always make sense, but once they form, they can be very difficult to dislodge. You develop a sort of "play it safe" mentality that caters to your fears rather than the actions that will help you thrive and nurture self-confidence, such as speaking up when someone acts unfairly or traveling to a new place full of possibility. Confidence in yourself, belief in your inner strength, is a part of self-love that's held out of reach by fear. Of course, there are therapies available to help diminish your fears, but there are also ways you can work around fear in your day-to-day. For example, you might have anxiety around the idea of a big party, but a gathering of three or four people is perfectly okay. Organize smaller events to nurture relationships and set a boundary around what you aren't comfortable with. Maybe you're afraid of flying, so you make long-distance travel a fun road trip with your favorite music and intriguing stops along the way. Finding ways to work around fear rather than allowing it to consume your life is a great act of self-love. You are demonstrating that you are worthy of success and happiness and accepting your differences instead of viewing them as a reason to not love yourself. Fears and phobias can be diminished over time and through effort, but you cannot put self-love on hold in the mistaken belief that you are undeserving until fearless.

TAKING ACTION

You may have some habits of your own that are rooted in fear and hold you back from doing things that can help you live a fuller, happier life. You may also have a loophole or workaround that lets you live your life even with fear lingering in the background. Think about some of the times you successfully outsmarted a fear. How did you work around these fears or even make them work for you? How might you use these experiences to get around fears or phobias moving forward?

Embrace Humanity

*There is no exercise better for the heart than
reaching down and lifting people up.*

—John Holmes, poet

You may sometimes feel undervalued at work or in society at large.
Maybe you've felt unseen by your employer or disrespected by your peers
lately. This sense of disregard plays into your internal dissatisfaction with
your life and yourself. When you feel others don't value you, you can
begin to question whether you are worth valuing. People will also pick up
on this self-doubt, giving you the lessened respect and appreciation you
present yourself as deserving. It is a hurtful cycle of diminished self-love.
Fortunately, you can break free from this cycle simply by extending kindness to others. As you come out of your shell to treat people as human
beings—to think beyond the idea of an employee or contractor serving a
customer or client and more in the sense of a genuine interaction—they
will naturally begin to do the same for you. You can practice showing

kindness for others everywhere, from the grocery store to the gas station to your office. These encounters don't always have to take place face-to-face, either. You can practice greater humanity and compassion in online interactions as well. Your inner and outer lives improve when you take a humane attitude toward what you do and how you act, both at work and in your free time.

TAKING ACTION

Take your next encounter, on or off the job: See if you can humanize the experience by paying your full attention, being present, and acting with kindness. For example, you might ask someone how their day is going or engage in other small talk rather than just giving a cursory smile and nod.

Choose Gratitude

No one says we must feel the gratitude.
Just recognizing the blessings in our lives
makes room for more of the good stuff.

—Susan B., author of *Getting Out from Going Under:*
Daily Reader for Compulsive Debtors and Spenders

Some days, you may struggle to find the good in the world. This stirs up a sense of deflation and discouragement that begins with other people and situations but eventually reflects back onto your view of yourself. If you can't find the good in the world, it can be equally difficult to find the good in yourself and in your life. Feeling a sense of hopelessness is a normal experience that most people have at some point in their lives. Fortunately, today's technology means it's not difficult to find news stories about people helping their neighbors, doing cool creative projects, and rescuing abandoned animals. You'll probably never answer the riddle of whether human nature is good or bad, but you can decide for yourself to focus on and be grateful for the people and events that *are* good. You can purposely look for the positives and try to magnify them even more through your personal interactions. You can buy a friend a gift to cheer them up, redecorate a corner of your home, or make a list of people you admire. When you brighten the world around you, you find that your inner landscape shifts as well. You feel more positive about yourself as you draw out positivity in your surroundings.

TAKING ACTION

Make a list of five things that make you feel grateful right now. If you're finding this difficult, think smaller: You can be grateful for a good cup of coffee, for *not* getting a traffic ticket, or for finishing a report at work. Repeat this exercise regularly.

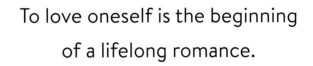

To love oneself is the beginning
of a lifelong romance.

—Oscar Wilde, author of *An Ideal Husband*

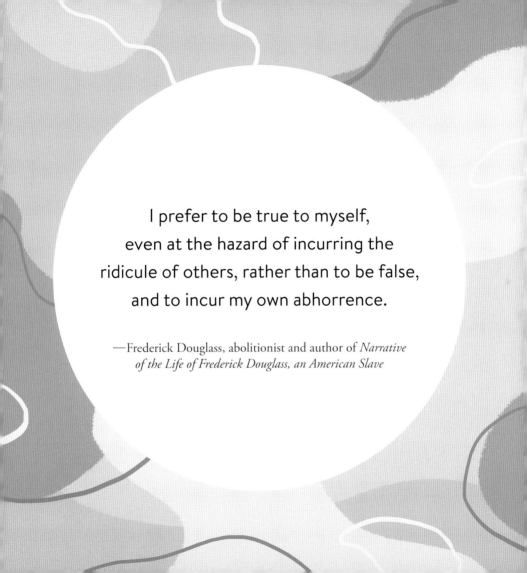

I prefer to be true to myself,
even at the hazard of incurring the
ridicule of others, rather than to be false,
and to incur my own abhorrence.

—Frederick Douglass, abolitionist and author of *Narrative
of the Life of Frederick Douglass, an American Slave*

Pleasure Yourself

Our bodies are where self-esteem,
desire, and sexuality come together.
The more attention we pay to our needs,
the better we are able to take care of ourselves.

—Miriam Kaufman, Cory Silverberg, and Fran Odette,
authors of *The Ultimate Guide to Sex and Disability: For All of*
Us Who Live with Disabilities, Chronic Pain, and Illness

If your love life is lacking at the moment, become your own lover. Take yourself on a date to a nice restaurant, buy yourself flowers, write yourself a love note, and yes, have a sensual night solo. When you give yourself pleasure, you send yourself a message that your own satisfaction matters. Even if you're in a long-term relationship, that's no reason you can't take care of yourself. In fact, engaging in eroticism for one can also help keep things spicy with a partner. You become more aware of what gets you going and the specific fantasies that appeal to you. Fantasizing sets the stage for the kinds of energies you want to bring into your real life.

Allow yourself some pleasure: It is one of the primary aims of life. There is nothing wrong with sensuality, and, by getting in touch with your passionate side, you demonstrate love for yourself.

TAKING ACTION

Imagine you are going on a second date with a special someone. What sort of gift would you buy that person? How would you show them you care? Now do that same thing for yourself.

Create a Positive Feedback Loop

Take a step back. Retreat, even for a few silent, quiet moments. Allow yourself to embrace the reality that every single life form (human, plant, animal) are embodiments of the sacred miracle of life. Allow yourself to relax into the truth that you are sacred as well. The way to manifest your sacredness is to embody sacredness—to treat all life as sacred.

—Cat J. Zavis, executive director, Network of Spiritual Progressives

Something magical happens in the space between effort and surrender. You need both parts—practicing daily disciplines and allowing the results to take care of themselves. Daily disciplines can be practices like mindfulness meditation, physical exercise, positive self-talk, or self-care rituals. When you honor and respect yourself, you begin to truly believe that you are deserving of honor and respect. The resulting love for yourself seems to fall into place naturally. This cycle of directing positive actions toward yourself and feeling positively about yourself only to direct those feelings back into more positive actions is known as a positive feedback loop. It doesn't matter where you begin in this loop. Whether you start with a positive feeling toward yourself or a positive action, one will fall into the other. What *is* important is that you set the intention to spark this positive feedback loop at the start of your day so it can continue through everything you do.

TAKING ACTION

How can you show yourself, concretely, that you are serious about this self-love business, about taking control of your own positive feedback loop? Do something to demonstrate your care for yourself. The size of the action does not matter so much as the symbolism behind it. Make yourself feel valued, whether through making yourself a nice cup of tea or taking a long lunch.

Tune In to the Rhythm of Reality

The same stream of life that runs through my veins night and day runs through the world and dances in rhythmic measures. It is the same life that shoots in joy through the dust of the earth in numberless blades of grass and breaks into tumultuous waves of leaves and flowers.

—Rabindranath Tagore, poet

At the beginning of an orchestral performance, the musicians all warm up their instruments in a cacophony of strings and brass, percussion and wind; then the conductor taps his or her baton against the music stand, the first violin plays an A, and the rest of the orchestra tunes to that note. By listening to that one note, all the musicians can sound their best, not just on their own but also as a group. You have to find that tuning note in your own life—the centering practice that helps you harmonize with the other people around you, to create the positive conditions of communication, teamwork, and more in your environment that allow self-love to flourish. This all begins with sitting still and listening, interjecting moments of quiet contemplation into your day so you can attune yourself to your surroundings. Steal bits of time from your schedule to do this whenever you feel out of sync with the people or situations around you. Go outside or enjoy a moment of quiet during your lunch break.

TAKING ACTION

Today, try a media fast. This can last for the next hour or the remainder of your day, depending on what's most feasible for you. See what it feels like to sit quietly in nature, to have a genuine conversation, or to work uninterrupted. When you feel tempted by entertainment or noise, take a ten-minute break of complete silence. Set a timer if necessary.

Get Out of the Defensive Crouch

Operating from a place of fear, we buy the belief that I've got to look out for me and mine because no one else will. *We lose our faith and stop trusting that Spirit will look after us. We become disconnected from other people, from ourselves, and from the sacred; and we perceive that we're on our own. We forget the great resources available to us when we're in touch with the divine.*

—Alberto Villoldo, medical anthropologist and author of
The Four Insights: Wisdom, Power, and Grace of the Earthkeepers

The pill bug, also called the roly-poly, will curl into a ball when it feels threatened. In similar situations of distress, opossums will play dead and turtles will retreat into their shells. The defensive crouch is common among animals, including humans. Times of adversity can lead you to withdraw into yourself, hiding from the outside world. This kind of duck and cover routine can persist even after the danger has passed; like any habit, it becomes second nature through repeated practice. While this survival instinct can be useful in the face of true threats to your life, giving it rein over everyday moments also means giving power to self-doubt. It means letting go of confidence in yourself and your abilities and allowing opportunities for joy to pass you by. It takes a lot of work to undo learned defensive behavior, to take chances again and brave the world. However, when that shift toward courage takes place, suddenly the world doesn't seem so hostile and uncaring, and you realize just how capable you can be in turbulent times. Coming out of your defensive crouch creates a sense of empowerment and ultimately a love of yourself and what you are capable of.

TAKING ACTION

You may have some situations in your life that cause you to hunker down and avoid other people. Maybe this habit has become ingrained over time. Consider these situations and the defensive stance you take and see if you can work against this tendency today.

Buy Less, Love More

Any intelligent fool can make things bigger, more complex,
and more violent. It takes a touch of genius—and a
lot of courage—to move in the opposite direction.

—E.F. Schumacher, statistician and economist

You may hear the constant drumbeat from society to buy more. From magazines to social media advertisements, the allure of materials and the exciting lives of others tempt you from every angle. And it can be easy in this beautiful, edited picture of a happy life to buy into the notion that you always need more than you have now—that this growth in possessions is the natural state of the world. These things will make you happy, make you more deserving of admiration and love…right? Then you run smack into the wall of reality; your bank balance is running out and you still don't feel as though you measure up. You still feel you don't have the right things to be "worthy." To truly love yourself, you must return to enjoying things as they are, to practice appreciating life with all its flaws and incompleteness. But accepting natural limits does not mean giving up. It opens a space of freedom in which you can *do more with what you already have*. You can make use of the materials at hand rather than consuming ever more. The love you cultivate for yourself in these moments is a love that can weather any ups and downs along the way. After all, objects can be lost, but the ability to be happy with what you have is a skill that you will carry—and that will carry *you*—through life.

TAKING ACTION

Look around your living space. How many things have you bought for some reason but never used? This could include an unopened bucket of paint, a book you haven't read, or a pair of shoes you've never taken out of the box. Consider why you bought these items and whether they are important to your happiness now. If not, let them go.

Listen to Your Intuition

The more you listen to your heart and trust that the universe has your best interests in mind, the more confident you will be in your decisions. Intuition is like a muscle: the more you use it, the stronger and more reliable it becomes.

—Molly Carroll, therapist and author of *Trust Within: Letting Intuition Lead*

You have probably had intuitions about people and situations, when something didn't feel quite right or you sensed a hidden opportunity. Sometimes you just *know* things without being able to explain why. An inner voice or image points the way or holds you back from taking a desired course of action, or you just have a sense that a particular person is either safe or dangerous. You can't really control or summon these little nudges; you can only be open to the possibility of receiving their inner guidance. Intuition is a powerful form of knowledge—the spark that gets other ways of knowing started. Intuition can lead to investigation, research, and experimentation. It may spark action or inspire artistic creation. This inner voice can also guide you toward greater self-love: It leads you toward the people and experiences that will encourage healing, a deeper understanding of yourself, and more enjoyment of the things that make you feel good inside and out. But you must first pay attention to its promptings. Be ready for that first spark of insight and allow it to grow into a flame.

TAKING ACTION

When life gets hectic, you can have a hard time connecting with your intuitive experience. Your brain runs on full tilt, unable to separate the many messages you have to process all at once. Take some time now to open yourself back up to your intuition. Sit in complete silence for five, ten, or twenty minutes and focus on a feeling of love and kindness. If something should distract you, bring your attention back to that feeling.

Practice a Soft Touch

Lack of self-compassion manifests in a harsh and judgmental relationship with ourselves. Many people believe that unless they are critical and demanding of themselves, they will be failures, unworthy of recognition and undeserving of love....We're afraid that if we were to be gentle and kind to ourselves, to relax our grip, we might not accomplish anything at all.

—Thupten Jinpa, author of *A Fearless Heart: How the Courage to Be Compassionate Can Transform Our Lives*

To nurture greater self-love, you have to learn to practice physical gentleness. This may sound like a foreign concept, as you have likely become used to the message that being a successful and deserving human being comes from dog-eat-dog competition, ceaseless striving, and relentless pursuit. Begin to rewire this belief with the presupposition that you can do things another way. You don't have to claw your way to the top, to be vicious with yourself and others to prove yourself worthy. Your soft animal self wants comfort and warmth, feelings deeply entwined with love, and you cannot wait for the accomplishment of a big life goal to be gentle. You need these things today in order to create a sense of self-love. Loving yourself means being your own best friend. Experiment with becoming a source of warmth and comfort for yourself and others. You may need to use a more assertive approach from time to time—you do have teeth and claws—but the competitive aspect is no longer a core purpose. You can save your fighting instincts for the right time and place. In the meantime, kind companionship with yourself builds a sense of self-love that will last.

TAKING ACTION

Take the time to get really cozy today. Try brewing yourself some herbal tea and curling up with a book and a blanket. Allow your worries to fade and spend some time quietly enjoying life in comfort.

Find Your Strength

*I was always looking outside myself for strength and
confidence, but it comes from within. It is there all the time.*

—Anna Freud, psychoanalyst

Society can often encourage a dualistic view of the world and those
within it: the self and the other, insiders versus outsiders, good and evil.
This zero-sum game of winners and losers rips the world apart. It cannot
be the case that humanity should be neatly divided between opposing
camps with clear lines of division. This belief only serves to close us off
from the lessons and experiences that others have to offer. To constantly
judge yourself on this win-lose scale diminishes self-confidence in favor
of greater self-doubt. Self-love requires that you find the strength to practice peace both with yourself and others. Does this mean you become a
pushover, ready to tolerate anything from aggressors? No. When you've
found the deep well of strength within, you overcome the petty bullies
of the world, without a lingering resentment that weighs on your mind

long after the situation has passed. You will also see yourself as a worthy ally, not an enemy to fight. You will be able to discern the best tactics for any situation. Importantly, peace should not be confused with weakness or passivity. The discipline you build in daily practice makes you ready to tackle any challenge and believe in your own ability to take on the twists and turns of life.

TAKING ACTION

You may find yourself facing internal enemies, like self-criticism and self-blame, or you may face external enemies, like an overbearing supervisor or a stingy landlord. You find relief from these difficulties when you face them directly. Imagine a difficulty you're currently dealing with. Now tap in to feelings of love and peace. Once they are concrete enough, aim them toward your trouble. Hold that loving frame of mind for at least ten to twenty minutes, then see if new solutions present themselves.

Express Your Emotions

Negative emotions are not bad. They're human. Much of the time they are situationally appropriate....The only truly negative emotions are emotions that you won't allow yourself or someone else to experience. Negative emotions won't harm you if you express them appropriately and then let them go.

—Joan Borysenko, scientist and author of
Minding the Body, Mending the Mind

You may have been conditioned to believe that negative emotions, anger especially, should be avoided, or at least kept inside, at all costs. But, of course, you can't get rid of anger or sadness or shame by wishing it away or ignoring it. It will only fester within and multiply. You harm yourself when you go for too long without any form of emotional release. This is when you find yourself unable to function. Your mind is taken over by a heavy feeling and it spills over into everything, from your ability to sleep soundly to your interactions with others. It also affects your relationship with yourself. The negativity you feel for the person or situation that sparked the emotion eventually turns around to reflect on how you view yourself. Self-doubt may also creep in, as you relive the past over and over, dissecting every word and action until you're unsure who is to blame. You don't need to let your emotions build up like this. You can avoid a breakdown through healthy, regular release. You may be able to express yourself in a conversation to resolve the problem or just vent to someone you trust. You can play music, draw pictures, write in a journal, do physical exercise, or use any other positive outlet. Taking care of your emotions is a simple form of self-love. When you get in touch with your feelings and work your way through them, your whole life works more harmoniously.

TAKING ACTION

If you are not comfortable talking about your feelings, try writing them down. Get some blank paper and write until you've described what's bothering you as completely and accurately as possible. Keep alert for the rest of the day. You may unexpectedly receive some guidance about your problem.

Declare a Ceasefire with Yourself

Self-love is not an end point or a destination that we arrive at after some kind of magical epiphany or surgical intervention. It's not a switch that gets flipped on, a product to be assembled, or a finish line that we cross. Instead, it's better to think of self-love as an ongoing process, a skill that we learn or a muscle that we strengthen over time.

—Sam Dylan Finch, writer and editor

Life gets easier when you no longer wage war within yourself. Perhaps you are struggling with a desire to be thinner or more successful. Maybe you're fighting against a disability or you simply lash out at yourself over every perceived imperfection. Self-love leads to healthier habits, being able to fight the situations worth your efforts, and seeking out life-affirming, joyful ways of existing in the world. You cannot wait until some ideal time in the future when conditions will align perfectly. You have to start the process of loving yourself *today*, by living as your true self in a world that may sometimes aim to hold you back. Everything hinges on that moment of internal resolve, in deciding to stop the inner battle and declare a ceasefire with yourself. Love and healing are possible for you today; you just have to lay down your weapons of self-harm and say yes to yourself and your life.

TAKING ACTION

Get out a journal or a sheet of blank paper and follow this prompt: "I commit to loving and taking care of myself in a sustainable way by _____." See if you can write at least one or two paragraphs' worth of ideas for increasing your self-love. Once you've finished writing, highlight or underline the action items and schedule them in your daily planner or your phone's calendar.

Make Peace with Your Mistakes

Loving yourself doesn't mean you think you're the smartest, most talented, and most beautiful person in the world. Instead, when you love yourself, you accept your so-called weaknesses, appreciate these so-called shortcomings as something that makes you who you are. When you love yourself, you have compassion for yourself.

—Andrea Brandt, psychologist

Make peace with all that you have done and left undone. Accept everything that has happened and the relationships that have ended or altered over the years. Making peace doesn't require you to do anything at all—it just shifts the way you perceive things. As you make peace with your past mistakes, you make it easier for self-love to take root. You stop blaming yourself for what you should or could have done. You stop looking with shame or regret on this or that mistake. You're able to stop exploring the what-if scenarios. Perhaps you wouldn't have made a mistake if you had done or said something different—perhaps life would be positively altered by taking back an error—but perhaps you would have missed out on a lesson learned. Or maybe that one thing needed to fall apart so better things could come together in the future. As you forgive your mistakes with this loving intent, the past has less of a grip on you. You're free to finally and confidently be yourself.

TAKING ACTION

Every time a little thing goes wrong today, take it as an opportunity to practice self-love. Repeat to yourself "I love you. I love you. I love you. I love you," or simply "love, love, love, love." You spill coffee on yourself. Love. You accidentally cut someone off in traffic. Love. You make a mistake at work. Love. Try it, just for today, and see what happens.

Set a Table for Love

You have one glorious and brief shot at being the you that is you on planet Earth, and the power to create whatever reality you desire. Why not be the biggest, happiest, most generous, and fully realized humanoid you can be?

—Jen Sincero, author of *You Are a Badass at Making Money: Master the Mindset of Wealth*

Love acts with extravagance. It gives unearned access to an unseen reward. It furnishes an inner mansion that has yet to be built. It makes its way into the hidden recesses of the heart, decorating its niches and walls with garlands of flowers. It lights a thousand lamps in the dark, dispelling the gloom. Where one person has dared to love, revelers will dance, sing, and play. Love cannot be stopped by ill fortune, sickness, or death. Love sees beauty wherever it goes and sings of its beloved. It echoes, immortal, through the ages, making noble everyone it touches. As the oldest and strongest force, love cannot be controlled. You can only ask it to enter, again and again. And because it is so kind and generous, it always comes when asked. Imagine yourself setting the table for self-love in your own heart and mind. Make a place card and decorate it with all the warm, welcoming elements that would make any guest feel at home. Once you've invited self-love into your life, start preparing the feast.

TAKING ACTION

Love comes in many different forms. It can be the warmth of friendship, the heat of romance, compassion for a stranger, or the fellow feeling of citizenship. Be on the lookout for love today, whether in your own heart or observed in others. Try to find at least three instances of love as you go through your day. As you note love in the world around you, try to direct those positive feelings inward. See how acknowledging different forms of love affects the way you feel about both others and yourself.

Be Your Own Cheerleader

Self-love is a journey.
It takes dedication, devotion, and practice.
Resolve to love yourself each and every day and
watch your best self blossom and
your greatest life unfold!
Self-love is an exponential force.

—Joyce Marter, psychotherapist

People are often very sparing in praising themselves. Few give themselves enough credit for their triumphs, gifts, and abilities. While modesty is an admirable quality, there is something more than modesty about this mindset: It's a neglect of yourself. You ignore or even discount your achievements and the wonderful qualities within yourself, instead opening that space to what you *haven't* achieved or the traits you *don't* possess. Every time you criticize yourself, you make it that much harder to achieve self-love, harder for your talents to reach their full expression. The way out of this trap is to consistently praise your own work to yourself. Do this whether you feel like it or not. Praise yourself frequently in the way you routinely brush your teeth or take out the recycling. The feelings of confidence and pride in yourself will come as you continue this practice.

TAKING ACTION

Today, practice being your own cheerleader. Every time you do something, say encouraging things to yourself. Give yourself little compliments such as "You did a great job on that" and "You look really nice today." This may feel silly at first, but keep at it! Try to maintain an encouraging voice throughout the day.

Get Into Motion

Nourishing yourself in a way that helps you blossom in the direction you want to go is attainable, and you are worth the effort.

—Deborah Day, mental health counselor

Spending so much time behind the wheel of a car or sitting behind a desk can make you lose touch with your physical body and its needs. Bodies want to be moving in their surroundings. We're made for action that requires more than the pressing of computer keys. Part of loving yourself means honoring your nature as an embodied being with a need to explore your surroundings and move to the full extent of your ability. Your mind also works much better when you get up and move, even for just a few minutes at a time. A bit of motion can help you expel negative self-talk and recenter on kindness toward yourself. Enjoying a breeze outside or stepping away from your desk to look out the window is enough to nourish your body's need for activity, refresh your mind, and show yourself that you are deserving of loving care.

TAKING ACTION
Take some time today to get up and move around, even if it's just doing some light stretching. Set yourself a reminder on your phone or computer so you don't forget.

Bank the Fire

Now each person has, by being this person,
his or her own unrepeatable beauty....
Whoever catches sight of this unrepeatable
value in me and is moved to love by what he sees,
loves me—not my qualities, not my excellences,
but me myself.

—John F. Crosby, contributor to *Ethical Personalism*,
edited by Cheikh Mbacke Gueye

Some have a fireplace in their home, whether a hearth set into the wall that burns wood or the gas-burning kind with fake logs. No matter the type of fireplace used, the fire is real, and it creates a cozy feeling, what the Danish call *hygge*. You can watch movies as a family, read a good book, or enjoy a craft while feeling warm and snug. In the olden days, to bank a fire meant to surround it with stones so the fire would be protected and there would still be enough heat in the embers to restart the fire the next morning. That's what you have to do with self-love: Regularly bank the fire of affection for yourself and surround yourself with its rosy glow so you are filled with a sense of cozy comfort even when the outside world begins to feel cold. It is so much more pleasant to live and work by the light of this fire of self-love. This fire is also portable. Through simple visualization you can stoke it whenever you want—just imagine piling up more stones of kindness and gratitude around your heart.

TAKING ACTION

Find some small way today to bank your fire of self-love through a kind act. It could be something simple like buying a nice pen or making yourself a good meal. Commit yourself to daily acts that keep your heart warm and grow your sense of love for yourself.

Build for the Future

The fault...is not in our stars,
but in ourselves,
that we are underlings.

—William Shakespeare, author of *Julius Caesar*

Your visions for the future rarely proceed as planned. This can leave you feeling adrift and out of sorts, not knowing what to do next. You may blame yourself for these unexpected twists or for taking what you perceive to be the wrong course of action. Time advances, and it can be a friend or foe of your journey to greater self-love depending how you make use of it. Prepare the tools you will need for the inevitable ups and downs in life in order to navigate them with love. Establish a support system of trusted friends and/or family members you can turn to, as well as a counselor or other professional mentor if you choose. Have a list ready of your favorite self-care activities, uplifting songs, and empowering mantras. Build up your own special toolbox of self-love to take out whenever you're in need.

The future does not have to be like the past: You can have a joyful life of confidence in and appreciation for your wonderfully unique self. It all begins with giving yourself the message that you are worth the effort.

TAKING ACTION

Take some time to tackle part of your self-love toolbox now. Make a list of self-care activities that make you feel pampered and deserving of kindness. Create your mood-boosting playlist. Talk to a loved one about possibly turning to them for support in the future. Bookmark lessons or activities in this book that you've found most helpful to flip back to at a later date.

Slow Down

It's an irony of our modern lives that while technology is continually invented that saves us time, we use that time to do more and more things, and so our lives are more fast-paced and hectic than ever.

—Leo Babauta, blogger

Contrary to popular belief, the world will not fall apart if you move at a slower pace and take the time to do things right the first time around. Rushing through life so often creates more problems than it solves, not to mention the added pressure of trying to do everything right away (and perfectly from the start). This race through time also impacts how you view yourself. The unnecessary expectation you place on yourself to hurry and always focus on the future makes it difficult to recognize and appreciate all the wonderful things about who you are and the life you lead right now. Instead, you think of only what comes next, of how you can do and be better moving forward. You discount your present self. To nurture greater self-love, practice moving slowly and deliberately through the world. Refuse the doubts and anxiety that come with rushed work. You will see that faster does not always equal better, and you will be able to savor your life instead of always being in a hurry. You'll feel a sense of empowerment and self-respect by taking back control over your time and setting your own pace. You'll be able to grow your self-confidence by doing one thing at a time well rather than doing twenty things at a time poorly. Fewer mistakes will arise, your mind will be clearer, and your emotions will be more stable. Most importantly, you will be treating yourself with the love you deserve.

TAKING ACTION

What is it that gives you a feeling of urgency when it may not be necessary? Is it driving through traffic? An approaching deadline? Perhaps even thinking about this situation makes you panicked. See the situation in your mind's eye while breathing very deeply and evenly. Invite a sense of peace into your heart while visualizing the situation. Repeat this exercise whenever the temptation to rush begins to rise.

Watch the Thoughts

Happiness doesn't depend on how
few negative thoughts you have, but on
what you do with the ones you have.

—Lisa Esile, author

Birds build their nests out of pine straw, twigs, and bits of string. They collect as they go, using the materials at hand (or beak). Your mind operates much like this, always collecting tidbits of information, gathering images and words and fashioning them into a little nest. You cannot turn off this impulse to collect any more than the bird can stop building its nest. When you close your eyes, you see the nest the mind has made for itself, a completely natural feathered lining of thoughts and memories gleaned from your surroundings. There is nothing wrong with this; it's simply something the mind does. Freedom comes from not judging. Imagine how silly it would be to criticize a bird for the way it builds its nest, and yet you likely criticize yourself all the time for having one thought or another. This constant criticism erodes your foundation of self-love. It builds on doubt and diminishes confidence. You can begin repairing this damage and cultivating love for yourself by allowing your mind to merely be, observing it without judgment.

TAKING ACTION

Practice watching your thoughts today. Note how your mind seems to light on one thing and then another, all on its own. You may sometimes see trivial thoughts flutter by. Try to avoid judging whatever arises. Simply watch, as though these thoughts don't even belong to you.

Play the Game of Life

*We just have to give experiences back to the world
and the people in it, in the same way that they
give them to us every day. That is how we happen
to life, and that is how we leave our mark. And,
in the end, isn't that what we're here to do?*

—Emily Bartran, writer and editor

You may think that life is some sort of problem to be solved, like a Rubik's Cube or a sudoku puzzle. You think you have to optimize this and maximize that, improve this and facilitate that in order to "win," but where exactly is this person who has won at life? Look at the lives of the rich and famous and you will rarely find anyone who truly has perfection. Instead, when you dig beyond the picturesque *Instagram* posts, you often find dysfunction. Rich and poor, religious and atheist, straight and queer—we are all human beings. There is no way to get it "right." There is no tutorial or instruction booklet for the game of life. All you can do is twist the cube this way and that, try things and see if they work. And you should give yourself a good bit of credit for simply trying to make things work, for trying to love yourself and others. The open-ended nature of life should also help you fret a little less. You didn't create this game; you're just playing it. Play it with loving intent and good things are sure to unfold.

TAKING ACTION

You may find yourself asking, "Why did this have to happen? Why me?" You may now be ready to let go of your expectations of the way things should be and instead become more at peace with the game as it is. Make a list of the ways your life is imperfect. Imagine what it would be like if it were okay for these things to be as they are, if you were playing the best that you could and your effort was enough.

Get Out of Your Own Way

Stop standing in your own way.
Stop making excuses.
Stop talking about why you can't.
Stop sabotaging yourself.
Decide which direction you are going in and take action.
One decision at a time, one moment at a time.

—Akiroq Brost, writer

Movement has an automaticity to it. When you get into the groove of life, things happen naturally. When you think too hard about things, always second-guessing yourself, things begin to feel difficult and self-love seems light-years away. You have to step back and let things happen, to get out of your own way. When you let go of the need to control a process, it simply unfolds without commentary. The obstacles fall away without any sort of inward or outward aggression. Once you learn this principle, your difficulties begin to loosen and the path to greater self-love becomes easier to travel. When things are not going well, when you feel a lack of confidence in yourself, take a break from trying to force things. The right guidance often comes when you set aside the need to predict the outcome or manipulate the situation.

TAKING ACTION

Do you have times when your work feels effortless, when things unfold naturally? See if you can get into this state for at least a few minutes today. If you're having trouble, view the work as simple manual labor. Think of your body as executing the task rather than your mind willing things to be done.

Your task is not to
seek for love, but merely to
seek and find all the barriers
within yourself that you
have built against it.

—Rumi, poet

When I loved myself enough,
I began leaving whatever wasn't healthy.
This meant people, jobs, my own beliefs
and habits—anything that kept me small.
My judgment called it disloyal.
Now I see it as self-loving.

—Kim McMillen, author of
When I Loved Myself Enough

Pick Your Battles

Choose your battles wisely.
After all, life isn't measured by
how many times you stood up to fight.
It's not winning battles that makes you happy,
but it's how many times you turned away and
chose to look into a better direction.
Life is too short to spend it on warring.
Fight only the most, most, most
important ones, let the rest go.

—C. Joybell C., author

You may sometimes have a hard time deciding which battles are worth fighting and which you should let go. Fighting them all saps your energy and leaves you feeling responsible for every little thing that goes wrong. And whenever you encounter resistance or are unable to change something, it can put your mind into a mode of self-blame and self-doubt, focusing on negative thoughts and feelings toward yourself that chip away at your self-esteem. A fight is worthwhile when it hinges on a principle you hold dear, when it allows you to hold on to an unalterable part of your identity, or when it uplifts and strengthens your community. Let go of most of the other stuff. It doesn't matter if someone cuts you off in traffic or talks about you behind your back. These are petty moments that will only leave you more frustrated in the end if you choose to fight. Conserve your energy for the fights that really matter, like when someone threatens your community or those you love. There are some struggles for which you were born; the rest are just annoyances.

TAKING ACTION

Have you ever had to fight for something when an important personal value was at stake? How did it feel to fight for something that truly mattered to you? Think of the battles you may have in your life right now. Choose one you feel strongly about and consider how you might approach it in an effective way, then release those lesser battles.

Demand Better for Yourself

*Responsibility to yourself means refusing to let others
do your thinking, talking, and naming for you; it means
learning to respect and use your own brains and instincts.*

—Adrienne Rich, poet

You may notice you sometimes apologize for feeling a certain way or for expressing how you feel. You may also notice you try to take up as little space in the world as possible, that you're overly afraid of bothering other people or of being a burden. You may avoid asking for help because you don't want to trouble anyone. You may not report poor service or ask for a refund because you don't want to seem rude or pushy. You may let people borrow things or you share your possessions to the point that you no longer get to enjoy them. You may feel uncomfortable with receiving gifts while being overly generous in giving them. All these traits are manifestations of holding yourself in low regard, of a lack of love for yourself, and you should be on the lookout for these behaviors. When you notice you're giving all of yourself away without receiving anything in return or you're apologizing for who you are, immediately begin to correct in the direction of higher self-regard. Demand better for yourself in all circumstances and you will find that you feel deserving of better.

TAKING ACTION
Think of a situation in your life that triggers nervousness or discomfort for you. Is it returning a poorly cooked meal at a restaurant? Saying no to something that exhausts you? Do one thing today to demand better treatment for yourself.

Let Frustration Be Your Fuel

I decided one day that I did matter, and the negative, hurtful ideals about who I am did not. If I wanted to love the person, body, and life I saw in the mirror, I had to stop internalizing the hatefulness of the world around me and start demanding that the world accepted my disability and personhood.

—Vilissa K. Thompson, disability advocate

Life may have dealt you a difficult hand in one way or another. Maybe you weren't born into a situation of privilege, or maybe you inherited a set of challenges over which you had no control. Maybe that feels unfair or makes you angry. If that's the case, let your frustration take you to new heights. Instead of turning inward and punishing yourself, channel your dissatisfaction into your work and personal life. Let your sense of injustice lead you to change your situation rather than resigning yourself to negativity. In order to love yourself, you cannot discount your feelings or decide to remain stuck in a situation that perpetuates low self-esteem. Self-love demands that you take all your pent-up energy and do something constructive with it. You have a right to shine as a person! You are entitled to make something of yourself, no matter your background.

TAKING ACTION

You most likely have something in your life that's made things difficult to one degree or another. Maybe you didn't have a lot of money growing up or you belong to a minority group. Maybe you have a disability or a chronic illness. The same things that make your life difficult are what make you unique as a person. Name some ways you can reframe your difficulties as positive powers. Use your frustration with these challenges to motivate you toward a change in perspective—and possibly a change in how you tackle life.

Release Your Guilt

An ethic built on caring strives to maintain the caring attitude....The source of ethical behavior is, then, in twin sentiments—one that feels directly for the other and one that feels for and with that best self.

—Nel Noddings, feminist educator and author of *Caring: A Relational Approach to Ethics and Moral Education*, second edition, updated

If you struggle with self-love, you may feel guilty about certain things. Maybe you feel bad for buying yourself a new pair of shoes, taking a long lunch break, or reading an entertaining but not necessarily esteemed novel. Guilt can be triggered needlessly or habitually when no actual wrong has occurred. It is a heavy yet sneaky emotion that creeps in solely to make you feel bad. Although guilt is sometimes necessary to keep the ego in check, a lot of the time it has less benevolent intentions. A part of loving yourself means letting go of unwarranted guilt. You owe it to yourself to extend the same courtesy to your own person that you would extend to others. If you wouldn't begrudge something to someone else, you shouldn't begrudge that same thing to yourself.

TAKING ACTION

Take a few minutes now for a simple meditation exercise for expelling guilt. Sit in a comfortable, quiet spot and focus on lengthening your breath, inhaling and exhaling fully. Feel your belly expand with each inhalation and contract with each exhalation. Each time you inhale, imagine your life force is being renewed and that greater love is coming to you. Each time you exhale, imagine you are releasing your feelings of guilt. Picture the guilt as a tangible thing being forced out of your body. Practice this meditation for at least five to ten minutes.

Push Your Limits

Don't limit your challenges. Challenge your limits.

—Jerry Dunn, marathoner

To love yourself fully, you must honor your inner need, your natural drive, to expand your potential. Think of sports like mountaineering or race car driving. Reason alone can't explain why such sports even exist— they certainly aren't practical or necessary—but they *do* exist because they appeal to our inner need to go beyond the previously attainable. You don't need to take such big risks to partake in the human desire to push beyond limits. You can love yourself more fully simply by pushing yourself to do your own absolute best. To avoid perfectionism, concentrate on one specific area of your life and make it something you can control, something that doesn't depend on a lot of outside factors. Set as your goal only one thing: to do better than you did before at that task. You can choose the benchmark that makes the most sense to you but make it something that will take time to achieve. When you push past your own limits, you gain a better sense of what you can achieve, and by intentionally giving yourself these wins, you restore a sense of faith and confidence in yourself.

TAKING ACTION

Choose a concrete way you can push past your own limits, something like improving your 5K time, making a certain number of sales calls, or writing for a certain amount of time each day. Make your goal higher than what you've done before but not so high that it feels daunting or impossible. Today, simply reflect on and write down your goal. Tomorrow, start making it happen.

Trust in Others

If one thinks of oneself as free, one is free, and
if one thinks of oneself as bound, one is bound.
Here this saying is true, "Thinking makes it so."

—Ashtavakra Gita, 1:11

You hold within your own heart the keys to the life you want. You have brilliant ideas and talents. The trouble lies in hiding your gifts from the world, in not trusting people to treat you fairly or act kindly toward these special parts of yourself. The path to self-love lies in opening yourself to others, in believing the world can be fair. You'll be able to show up for the people in your life on deeper levels and nurture stronger connections that feed your heart and soul. As you trust more in those around you and build more fulfilling relationships, you will also cultivate more confidence in yourself, both in the ways you can be of service to others and through the connections that lift you up. Today you can trust that, when you put yourself out into the world with faith, others will come alongside you to support your endeavors. No matter the disappointments of the past, know that your cocreators are waiting for you, wanting to take part in your initiatives and bring them through to completion.

TAKING ACTION
Are you having trouble trusting someone in your life? If you feel like the relationship is worth holding on to, try giving that person the benefit of the doubt. Either mentally or out loud, commit to giving the relationship a reset. Forget about the past and move forward with a fresh start.

Try a Little Introspection

It's weird, you get to a certain point in your life where it becomes clear what you love about life, what you really enjoy about life and what you don't....So you just lean into stuff that you like. It's about finding joy in life.

—David Arquette, actor

Picture a big, tangled ball of yarn. That's what the self is like. It's a mess of different strands—thoughts, emotions, memories, all the mental aspects of yourself—going here, there, and everywhere. To untangle the yarn, to understand yourself, you have to follow the threads through your heart and mind. At the same time, you may not have access to the whole tangle at once; you have to follow the threads that are available to you. You have to take what you do know and use that to find your way through the unknown parts of yourself. An important part of loving yourself involves this self-exploration, learning the ins and outs of your own personality and motivations so that you can build more confidence in these different elements of yourself. The work of introspection gives you tremendous emotional intelligence that you can use to understand yourself and ultimately your whole world. Then you'll be better prepared to live the life that gives you the greatest satisfaction.

TAKING ACTION

Today, make some lists to better capture what it's like to be you. To start your introspective journey, try beginning with these prompts: "The five most important things in life to me are...," "The five activities that bring me the most joy are...," and "It really bothers me when people do these five things..."

Find Your Balance Between Sociability and Solitude

What I am dealing with over and over
is having your ease in the world pulled out from
under you, because I don't feel easy in the world.
The flip side of that, the positive side of that,
is that it makes a clearing where you can
see the world with fresh eyes,
see the world with a sense of wonder.

—Judy Fiskin, photographer

Most of us have had the feeling that we don't belong at one time or another, like we're not part of the in-crowd or not really like other people. This kind of social disconnect may become a source of low self-esteem if left unchecked. On the other hand, if you're constantly forcing yourself to socialize and connect with others, it can build up a belief that a need for solitude is not okay and therefore there might be something "wrong" with you for feeling exhausted after an event or meetup or for simply wanting some time to yourself. You may find yourself alternating between the need to be around other people and the desire for solitude, and neither path is innately right or wrong. What is important is feeling like you're getting what you need from life. If you're feeling deprived of either social or alone time, find a way to get what you need, if only for a few minutes per day. For a more introverted person, sitting in a public place like a park or a restaurant can be people time, while for an extrovert that same activity could count as solitude. Wherever you fall on that spectrum, make sure you strike a balance that feels right for you.

TAKING ACTION

Are you feeling like you need to be around people more often, or perhaps like you need more time to yourself? See if you can take at least a few minutes today to push yourself in the direction your internal needs are pulling you toward.

Take a Midday Reset

Better do your own task imperfectly
than do another's well.
Better die in your own duty.
Another's task brings peril.

—Bhagavad Gita, 3:35

A simple strategy that you can use to manifest more self-love is to take a midday reset. Sometimes a day just goes off the rails: you wake up on the wrong side of the bed, spill your coffee on yourself, or the day just generally feels negative. It's enough to shake your confidence and doubt your life. In the middle of the day, pause to have some sustenance and do some deep breathing. Then say to yourself, "I love you, no matter what happens today. I love you, no matter what you accomplish or don't accomplish today." When you return to your work or personal life, attend to things with this unconditional acceptance of yourself. You'll find some of the pressure has been released and you're able to relax a little more.

TAKING ACTION

See if you can identify a time when you can take a few minutes for yourself in the middle of the day. Maybe you can take five minutes on your lunch break or in between errands. You can sit in your car or your house if you like—you just need a few quiet minutes to do your own midday reset. If not today, put it on your schedule for tomorrow.

Steer Your Inner Landscape

Teach her to reject likeability. Her job is not to make herself likeable, her job is to be her full self, a self that is honest and aware of the equal humanity of other people.

—Chimamanda Ngozi Adichie, author of *Dear Ijeawele, or a Feminist Manifesto in Fifteen Suggestions*

You have come to the end of a long day. Your body feels tired, and your mind is on the edge of coming unglued. The last thing you want is to give yourself something else to do, yet sometimes you close your eyes at night and find only worries: about the events in the news, the bills you have to pay, and a million other things. When this happens, try to recall the patterns on your grandmother's quilts. Think of the apple tree you climbed as a kid. See if you can name all the streets in your hometown or all the teams in the American and National Leagues. If none of that works, read a book of very dry economic theory. Your goal is to give your mind enough to do that it doesn't chase after every stressor but not so much that it conjures new calamities. Make your mental rituals particular to you, to the landscapes of your own life. You alone govern your mind. Engaging in these mental rituals and taking charge of your interior landscape is a simple act of self-love that allows you to give yourself the rest that you so desperately need. Then you can work from a place of calm and clarity instead of always going full throttle.

TAKING ACTION

Take the time to do some deep breathing. Try breathing in for four counts and breathing out for four counts. It's preferable to breathe through the nose as nostril breathing slows the breath and makes it more deliberate. You may also try saying a power word on the inhale, like "peace" or "calm." Or, if you have an uplifting mantra, you can practice timing it to your breath.

Allow Feelings to Run Their Course

Feel, he told himself,
feel, feel, feel.
Even if what you feel is pain,
only let yourself feel.

—P.D. James, author of *The Children of Men*

As a society, we have gotten used to the idea that the solutions to our problems are just a click away. We can order takeout for dinner, buy a new piece of furniture, or access any material thing or piece of information without having to leave our beds, but instant gratification doesn't take care of the problems of the spirit. You can only come to know yourself as a person—to appreciate all that you are—by looking inward and watching the emotions that flow through you each day without attempting to force them one way or another. When you sit still with your feelings, whatever they may be at that moment, you find a calm within the storm. You recognize how fleeting emotions are, how they twist and turn and naturally run their own course. You can appreciate each one for what they offer and for their temporary nature rather than trying to control or repress them. Attempting to force your emotions, when they inevitably ebb and flow in their own design, only leaves you feeling negatively about yourself. Take control of your self-love by *letting go* of control, by giving your emotions the space they need to run their course.

TAKING ACTION

Watch your troubles closely and they go away. It may seem impossible at first but give it a try. Take whatever might be bothering you and deeply observe the emotions that come with it. See what triggers those feelings and what makes them continue. Get extremely familiar with your distressing emotional patterns so you know them like the back of your hand. Each time you observe closely, negative feelings have a little less power over you. Give it a try for just ten or fifteen minutes today.

Grow Through All Seasons

In nature, nothing is perfect
and everything is perfect.
Trees can be contorted,
bent in weird ways,
and they're still beautiful.

—Alice Walker, Pulitzer Prize–winning author

I have a camellia bush in my yard that blooms twice a year, winter and summer, dropping pink blooms the size of saucers. I have never given it fertilizer or pruned it; the camellia just keeps blooming and growing in sandy soil through droughts and storms. Humans can learn a lot from plants, from how they grow dependably, year after year, asking for little from us yet providing so much. A plant never asks for more than it needs, and it uses the good years to balance the bad. Sometimes you may take setbacks personally, which only prolongs the recovery. You may also tend to wait for perfect conditions instead of going ahead with what you've got. Like plants, self-love doesn't wallow in a state of lacking and deprivation. It proceeds along its path no matter how limited its resources are. It finds abundance in all conditions. Tune in to the lessons of nature's rooted gifts and use their wisdom to motivate you along your journey to greater self-love.

TAKING ACTION

As you look back on your life, you'll see lots of ups and downs, good times and bad. If you inquire further still, you may find that your personal growth accelerates even amid the most difficult circumstances. Can you think of a time when things were not going well on the outside but you still gained life lessons that affect you to this day? Take a few minutes to write about this situation. What might you gain from the difficulties facing you now?

Find Your Body Balance

It took me many years to accept,
to fully internalize, that if someone can look at me
and tell that I am trans, that's not only okay—
that's beautiful, because trans is beautiful.
Trans is beautiful, and I am not beautiful despite
my big hands, my big feet, my wide shoulders,
my height, my deep voice, and all the things
that make me beautifully and noticeably trans.
I am beautiful because of those things.

—Laverne Cox, actress

The body is not the sum total of who you are, but it *is* an important aspect of your personhood. It can express your personality to the outside world, and it's the vessel that carries you from one day to the next. Your treatment of your body falls on a spectrum. On one side there is harsh treatment, like over- or undereating and extreme exercise regimens, while on the other side there is indifference and neglect, ignoring the body altogether. Self-love asks that you find a middle ground of physical self-care where you give your body diligent and kind attention. You try to eat a good diet, which doesn't necessarily mean counting every calorie or never eating a treat you love. You exercise without overtaxing yourself to the point of injury or unsustainability. You practice beauty regimens and wear select fashions, but you don't have to be on top of every trend or feel bad about throwing on a pair of sweats sometimes. You can have a sane, balanced life and still accept and love the way your body looks and feels. The body can be a friend if you give it balanced care and kindness.

TAKING ACTION

Think of a time when your embodiment (some aspect of your body or the way that it functions) was making you crazy. Write a few paragraphs about that experience. Maybe you struggled with an eating disorder or religion-based fasting. Maybe you went to the gym too often or your membership card sat collecting dust. Perhaps you have a certain part of your body that gives you self-doubt. Try to do something today to practice balanced kindness toward your body.

Ask the Big Questions

I am always looking and
I am always asking questions.

—Anne Rice, author

Our hearts hold queries, and we turn them over and over like an oyster turning a pearl. We try to smooth the rough edges of these questions but they never fully go away. "Why am I here?" "Is there a higher power?" "What is the best moral system?" These big, difficult questions give your life meaning even as you wish to be rid of them. They provide you with food for reflection and work if you allow them fully into your life. When you try to banish them altogether, life becomes mundane. And there is no one right answer to the big questions. There are many answers, and each of us approaches them in our own way. While you may not be able to answer these questions definitively for yourself, living with them gives your life a drive that fuels confidence and cultivates joy. For this reason, nurturing greater self-love requires experiments in living as it pertains to questions of ultimate meaning.

TAKING ACTION

What are the big questions in your life right now? Do you sometimes avoid these questions, or do you confront them directly? Write down one of your big questions and reflect on it for a while. Use paper or just let your mind wander.

Start Small

Willingness is...the antidote to helplessness, and, as such, the kernel of a kind of faith. You take one baby step, then another; you leap off this tiny cliff and that one; you keep it up long enough and somewhere along the way you begin to understand that moments of emptiness and despair can be survived, that pain can be offset by pleasure, that fear can give way to safety.

—Caroline Knapp, author of *Appetites: Why Women Want*

Loving yourself can feel like too much when you've gone through days, months, or even years of difficulty. The world may also feel like an unsafe place during these times, like you might get blasted at any moment by an unkind word, an unexpected bill, or some new catastrophe. To get past these heavy feelings and move forward in your journey to greater self-love, you have to start very small. Starting small could mean unloading the dishwasher, answering some emails, or taking a walk around the block. On bad days, it could mean taking a shower and getting dressed. Small victories lead to bigger victories. When you take care of yourself in these small ways, you become bolder in facing the world as you discover and build on your inner strength. Self-love grows as you develop your ability to take care of yourself and persevere through difficulty. You prove to yourself that you are worth nurturing—and you are capable of much more than you once believed. No matter what situations you may be dealing with, give yourself permission to take things slowly. This point in your journey is important in and of itself, so don't be in a rush to get ahead. Take your time and go at your own pace.

TAKING ACTION

Do you sometimes find yourself playing the comparison game, trying to see if someone in your life is doing better or worse than you are? Write a quick paragraph about what normally triggers you to start comparing and how that comparison game makes you feel. See if you can resolve to stop comparing your journey to those of other people.

Shed Your Skin

Although often depicted as the bad guy,
the deceptive, treacherous villain,
the snake is actually a beautiful
symbol of feminine power.

—Brigit Esselmont, author and professional tarot reader

The snake, when its skin feels tight and dry and too small for its growing body, will slither between stone and branch, sloughing off a translucent image of its former self. It must feel so good for the snake to unveil its shiny new scales. Cultures across the earth both venerate and fear the snake for its power. According to Hindu philosophy, every person in the world has the serpent power coiled within themselves, a strong Kundalini energy found at the base of the spine. This energy enables growth and leads you to shed your skin through each stage of growth. By tapping in to your own inner serpent power, you can find direction in life to become the confident, self-loving, and ultimately happy person you want to be.

This is not about becoming someone different but becoming the person you already are inside and growing into the power you already have.

TAKING ACTION

Write for a page or two about the areas in your life where you feel confined and dissatisfied, then write an equal or greater amount about what you can do to change your situation. Limit yourself to listing changes you can make right now, without any big infusion of resources, then get started right away. Allow your serpent power to bring you to greater love and fulfilment.

Embrace Healthy Risk

This idea of what you're going to transition into or who you're going to be—that's not how you're going to end up. You don't know who that person you're going to transition into is. You just have to see.

—Laura Jane Grace, musician and author

As humans, we are pulled by countervailing forces: One impulse wants stability and another wants change. Going with either force takes its toll on your sense of love for yourself and the life you lead, and the process of choosing may strain your relationships with others, sometimes to their breaking point. If you prioritize stability and reject any opportunities for change, life can end up feeling dreary and monotonous. There is no meaning to what you do; therefore, you may wonder if your self has meaning. If you prioritize change and dismiss all options for stability, life can lose its sense of mooring. You have no foundation to turn to when things get difficult, and thus it's even easier for self-doubt to take hold. For some, change feels too scary. It's a jump into the unknown where even the best-laid plans may not account for what actually happens. For others, fear lies in taking a chance on stability. Being secure might seem like a surrender to boredom for those who love change. However, each side of the coin holds opportunities for growth and discovery. Perhaps making a change leads to a fun new adventure, or creating a bit of stability in your life actually gives you more room to pursue your interests. Each is a risk, and loving yourself means embracing a healthy amount of risk, to act on faith in pursuit of your dreams. As you rely on yourself and your world through these risks, you build confidence and uproot self-doubt.

TAKING ACTION

In what places in your life do you feel the need for comfort and stability? In what areas do you feel the need to make big changes? Make two lists—one of areas in which you want stability and another of areas in which you want change—then go down each list and see which item feels most pressing and important to you. Which one of the items on the lists makes your heart leap with excitement or warmth? This exercise can provide you with a beginning point for exploring and expressing yourself.

Choose Your Affinities Carefully

Identification is, of course,
identification with an other,
which means that identity is
never identical to itself.

—Douglas Crimp, queer theorist

We make ourselves through a process of networking with people and groups with whom we identify socially, politically, religiously, or in some other relation. What is called the "self" is a network-in-process, a cobbled-together assemblage of affinities. When you form alliances through coercion, you experience fear and alienation. When you form alliances through love and respect, you experience satisfaction. It can be difficult to sort through your own motivations, to turn a spotlight on your choices to see why you choose particular affinities. Deep reflection allows you to understand the push and pull at work behind the scenes—the forces of attraction and repulsion that make you who you are.

Self-love means deliberately choosing the kind of affinities that will help you express yourself more fully and grow in the direction you would like to grow. Surround yourself with those who encourage you in your dreams and shine a light on what is worth loving about you. Avoid those who only make you question your worth.

TAKING ACTION

Make a list of your affinities: people you admire, your favorite places, the books and music you like, etc. Put it all together in the form of a big web diagram, with connections between the different parts. It might look like an investigation board in a detective movie by the end.

Increase the Intensity

Ambition is enthusiasm
with a purpose.

—Frank Tyger, editorial cartoonist

You may already be doing things that make you feel good about yourself, and if so, you're moving your life in a positive direction. (Maybe you've picked up a few habits since you started reading this book!) Think now about increasing the intensity—increasing your drive and the frequency of these loving practices. You can think of it like putting a pot on to boil. If you put the stove on medium-high, the water will eventually boil, but if you turn it all the way up to high, the water will boil much faster. Direct overwhelming love toward yourself in the same way. Give the best things to yourself that you can afford. Use your time in the best way possible. Increase your knowledge and gain new skills. Associate with good people. Get into good mental and physical habits. Love yourself like it matters, like it counts, because it does. The intensity of love you direct toward yourself now determines the kind of life you have the privilege of living.

Too many people overvalue
what they are not and
undervalue what they are.

—Malcolm Forbes, entrepreneur

You have been criticizing yourself
for years and it hasn't worked.
Try approving of yourself and
see what happens.

—Louise Hay, author of *You Can Heal Your Life*

Get Creative

You can't use up creativity.
The more you use,
the more you have.

—Maya Angelou, writer and civil rights activist

The creative impulse goes to the heart of who you are as a human being. You naturally want to make things, to bring something to light that has never been seen before. Creativity does not belong to some set of elite beings; it belongs to each and every one of us. When you create, you tap in to deep wells of story and symbol that help you understand who you are, both as an individual and as a member of a civilization. Something magical works through the materials themselves, through the paints, the musical instruments, the written words. When you open yourself to creation, strong currents move through you, making way for your artistic release. Making art returns you to yourself. In the creative process, you reveal your hidden self and cultivate an appreciation for your inner world and the abilities and uniqueness you may otherwise overlook.

TAKING ACTION

Take a few minutes today for artistic exploration. If you're intimidated by the thought of making art, think of it as doodling or scribbling. Put pen to paper, plonk away at a guitar, or do some cross-stitching. Your work doesn't have to be something profound. It can be silly, energetic, or any mood whatsoever. Forget about art in the gallery sense—just enjoy the experience.

Be Bold

*Be bold
in what you stand for
and careful
what you fall for.*

—Ruth Frankel Boorstin, librarian of Congress

When you embrace yourself with boldness and dare to declare your love, especially for yourself, your life has more space for expression and independence. How do you practice boldness? It begins with learning to say yes: yes to the face in the mirror, yes to your desires, and yes to the life you want to live. The yes of pleasure, self-acceptance, and community ends the isolation and pain of self-doubt and the denial of your wonderful self. When you dare to say yes, you make your life more full and complete. Your entombed self comes alive again, your senses awaken, and you see and feel delight all around—and within. Yes, yes, yes!

TAKING ACTION

Commit to being bold, just for today. Don't tone down your words or your voice. Don't hold back with your fashion choices or self-expression. Don't keep it all buttoned-up and buckled down. You've got this. Say yes to your whole self.

Ease Stress

The time to relax is when you don't have time for it.

—Sydney J. Harris, journalist

We denizens of the twenty-first century seem congenitally unable to relax, even for a few minutes. Think of your last vacation (if you can remember it). Were you really able to "get away from it all," or were you firing off emails while texting on your phone? The problem goes far deeper than increased connectivity via electronic gadgets or living in a hectic environment. Your psyche needs the validation of being important, of being needed. Stress itself has become a status symbol. If you're not stressed, there must be something wrong with you. You must not be pushing hard enough or making enough of your life. Self-love becomes possible only when you reject stress as a status symbol and embrace the life you want—when you're unafraid of being labeled as unproductive or lazy by others because you understand your happiness is the most important thing in life. You matter as a person, regardless of what you're doing or not doing. Loving yourself requires stepping back from the things that only serve to keep you in a constant state of anxiety. You must take time and space to realign with what is most important to you and to explore practices that can help you regularly ease stress.

TAKING ACTION

Today, take note of every time you feel pressured to be busy, whether out of fear you'll be judged for not being productive or because your own inner critic is telling you to go go go for fear of wasting the day. Try to ease that response a little. Place more focus on doing what you love. Ask, "Am I enjoying myself?"

Start Anew

We don't learn to love in a linear path, from self to family to friends to spouse, as we might have been taught. We learn to love by loving. We practice with each other, on ourselves, in all kinds of relationships. And right now we need to be in rigorous practice, because we can no longer afford to love people the way we've been loving them.

—Adrienne Maree Brown, writer and activist

You may have a hard time loving yourself because of a past hurt that's left a deep emotional (and possibly physical) wound. Maybe someone you loved left and you blame yourself. Perhaps a former friend hurt you intentionally and you still struggle to trust yourself in choosing friendships that won't turn malicious. These scars do not go away just because you wish they would. Experiences in childhood, relationships with family and friends, and numerous other factors all shape how you see not just the outside world but also yourself. Almost everyone has some sort of emotional damage, and the journey toward loving yourself—and others—requires healing old wounds that tether you to the past. You can learn to live more authentically by letting go of the past, even if you cannot forget it.

TAKING ACTION

Take a few minutes now to look at the possible damage in your own past. There may be a troubling episode in your life that you've never examined until now or that you haven't thought of in years and you may glean new insights as an older, more experienced person. Write about this time now. Describe what happened and consider how it has affected you through the years.

Be Kind

Compassion allows you to stop blaming yourself and instead understand yourself....True compassion can be powerful. Many people believe compassion is weakness— just making excuses or letting yourself off the hook—but it's not. You may be surprised to hear that greater compassion toward yourself leads to stronger motivation to change.

—Lisa M. Najavits, psychiatrist and author of *Finding Your Best Self, Revised Edition: Recovery from Addiction, Trauma, or Both*

Animal trainers and behavioralists teach that if you're trying to train a puppy not to pee on the carpet, it does no good to yell at the puppy or hit it with a newspaper. That only teaches the puppy to be afraid. A more productive method is to pay attention to the puppy to see when it needs to go to the bathroom and let it outside frequently. The puppy should then be rewarded for good behavior. This is known as positive reinforcement, and it works the same way for people, including yourself. If you are kind and understanding to yourself—if you listen to yourself and forgive your mistakes—you can accomplish so much more than you ever could with harsh judgments and blame. Through this simple act of self-love over self-criticism, you can get to know your inner motivations and what techniques actually work for achieving the things you want. Self-love is far more effective than the destructive ways of relating to yourself (self-harm, addiction, self-criticism, etc.) that you may have learned over the years. Practice the same basic kindness you would offer to others with the person you spend every minute of every day with: yourself.

TAKING ACTION

As you go through your day, practice small acts of kindnesses with yourself. Imagine saying "please" and "thank you" to yourself when you get things done. Give yourself a small treat when you complete a big task. Listen to some music or read a book you like.

Try Something New

When we try something new...
our brains and bodies are challenged.
Once stagnant or underused neurotransmitters
or muscles are shocked and put to use.
Our bodies and brains thrive on the attention,
and we feel better as we put them into practice.

—Allan Karl, author and photographer

You are never too old or too broke to explore something new. Part of treating yourself with the loving care you deserve means keeping life interesting, turning over a new leaf once in a while. You don't have to wait for a midlife crisis or until you retire to try something new, either. You can use any random Tuesday, rainy day, or summer afternoon to try out a pursuit. Keep in mind that whatever you try doesn't have to involve a career change or even be classified as a hobby; anything that stands out to you will be worthwhile. If you don't like it, you'll have an interesting story to tell and a deeper understanding of what doesn't work for you. If you *do* like it, you'll have one more thing that brings joy and a sense of fulfillment to your life.

TAKING ACTION

Today, reflect on a new pursuit you could try either now or in the near future. Start by making a list of all the things you've wanted to do but have yet to make time for. Maybe you'd love to go salsa dancing, play the accordion, or take a poetry class. Include at least one of these in your schedule for the day or week.

Act with Feeling

Self-love is not simply a state of feeling good.
It is a state of appreciation for oneself that
grows from actions *that support our physical,*
psychological, and spiritual growth.
Self-love is dynamic;
it grows through actions that mature us.

—Deborah Khoshaba, psychologist and author

To truly love yourself, you have to make self-supporting behaviors part of your daily routine. Every day there must be some loving practices to reinforce the idea that you are worthy of love. These practices could include eating a healthy meal, getting some physical exercise, doing meditation, reading a book, keeping track of finances, or anything that makes you feel like your life is in good order and on the right track. At the end of the day, you should be able to say to yourself, "I'm glad I did that. I really did myself a favor today." When the off days come—days when you don't do as much as you'd like or you still feel less than loving toward yourself—you shouldn't beat yourself up about it. Bumps in the road are a part of any journey, and tomorrow is a new opportunity to get back on track. What matters is that you continue forward with the intent to practice love and to make all your decisions from this intent.

TAKING ACTION

There may be times when you feel it's too late, that there have been too many setbacks or mistakes or hurt to bother trying now. Indeed, this is an easy trap of negative thinking to fall into, but you can pull yourself out of it. Consider this: What if today was the last day you had to live? What would you want to do to make it worth it? Make a list of four or five activities and pick one that is feasible right now. Go do it!

Focus On Today's Portion

*We can never destroy our natural creative potential;
we can only disconnect from it by blocking its flow
through us. This happens when we become adrift in
the fog of overwhelm, overwork, and
overidentifying with external measures of
success to define our internal sense of self.*

—Amy Beth Acker, psychotherapist and author of
*The Way of the Peaceful Woman: Awaken the Power of
You, Create a Life You Love, and Set Yourself Free*

When you become overwhelmed at the prospect of loving yourself, perhaps after years of neglect or harm, remember that you only have to take care of today's portion. Think about what loving yourself means for you today. It could mean making an appointment with your therapist, sitting and watching the birds in the front yard, or calling in sick if you don't feel well. Every person's life is different, and each day is different. You have to learn to listen to yourself and your own life to determine what is most necessary on this day. You need determination to nurture self-love, yes, but you also need flexibility so you become adaptable to each situation as it emerges. What may have been necessary or helpful in your journey yesterday may not be what is necessary or helpful today. So, what does today's portion require?

TAKING ACTION

Take a few minutes to listen to yourself and your life right now. Choose one thing you can do today to make yourself feel loved, then choose one thing to cut back on that you may have been overdoing or that isn't urgent. Fill that time with what makes you feel loved.

Follow Your Own Timeline

*Discovering the ways in which you are exceptional,
the particular path you are meant to follow, is your
business on this earth, whether you are afflicted
or not. It's just that the search takes on a special
urgency when you realize that you are mortal.*

—Bernie Siegel, physician and author of *Peace, Love, & Healing:
Bodymind Communication & the Path to Self-Healing: An Exploration*

Sometimes you might think of finding yourself as a youthful activity, as though you only need to find your direction once and then you're through, but the world changes every day—and you change with it. Each passing year brings new insights and it may also bring different likes and dislikes. Most people will reinvent themselves many times throughout their lives. The situations you may have thought were settled won't be so later in life, so you find yourself starting over again at different points. Despite this constant change, you have unique contributions to make to the world in each phase of your development. Of course, at each transition point, there can be a sense of purposelessness or despair before you understand these contributions, and self-love is very important in successfully finding your way through these moments. Self-love provides protection from feelings of doubt that can slow or even halt your transition into a new phase of life. Believing that you have something to contribute to the world gives you the confidence to move forward into the unknown.

TAKING ACTION

Make a quick timeline of your life on paper. What have been the major transition points thus far? What might be future transitions you encounter? You might include events like moving, getting married or divorced, changing jobs or careers, going to school, having children, or major accidents and illnesses. Making this timeline can give you a sense of how far you've come and where you are now. Be proud of your progress and the obstacles you've overcome.

Live for Love

*It's not that love falls
to the power of pain.
Rather, it's that pain is shaped
by power of love.*

—Craig D. Lounsbrough, professional counselor and author

You may be going through hard times right now. You may have lost a friend or family member, or you may have a difficult medical condition or financial issue. You may be facing discrimination or feeling despondent about the state of the world. Know that deep within your heart lies great resilience and strength. Love is powerful. It overcomes hate and hardship and has given countless others before you the ability to push forward. When doubt or sorrow creeps in to tell you that things aren't worth it, choose love. Set the intention to love others and allow that love to seep into how you treat yourself. Live for love, and love will see you through.

TAKING ACTION

The heart is the intersection of self and world, the nexus of transformation that lies within every person. Meditate on the heart. Allow each and every thing you love to appear in your heart. Silently ask for or explore ways to strengthen each love.

Make Time for Yourself

Maybe what we really need are fewer distractions and more focus. Maybe what we really need are a few carefully chosen constraints that narrow our energy onto what really matters rather than compiling a bunch of resources that pull us away from what we actually need to do.

It's very possible that eliminating distractions, not accumulating resources, is the best way to maximize your potential.

—James Clear, writer

Sometimes you may approach life in a militant way, focused on the responsibilities of each day. It feels like there is so much to do, both at work and at home, that taking the time to relax feels like a distraction from your duties. You might break out productivity apps and to-do lists, each day a struggle to stay ahead of or simply catch up to the curve. After all this attention to the things that *need* to get done, there's no time left for the things you *want* to do. Sometimes we have to set down the lists and say, "I am going to go kayaking/take a nap/play the guitar/bake some cookies," or whatever activity is purely for you. How many times have you put yourself last to satisfy your boss or family member or whoever, only to never pay yourself back for that lost time? How many times have you promised yourself time to do what you love, only to never get around to it? To practice self-love, you have to *make* yourself make time for the things you want to do. It has to become non-negotiable. You are worth it, and when you give yourself the time, you feel so much more energized and ready to take on those to-dos.

TAKING ACTION

Clear your schedule for at least half an hour today. Give yourself permission to do something you really want to do during that time. Let go of any guilt about devoting time to what you enjoy.

Don't Just Dream It, Be It

Knowledge does not mean mastering a great quantity of different information but understanding the nature of mind. This knowledge can penetrate each one of our thoughts and illuminate each one of our perceptions.

—Matthieu Ricard, writer and Buddhist monk

To cultivate real love for yourself, you have to stop living in the land of coulds and shoulds, of "I could be this" or "I should be that." For many, it's easy to become so caught up in the realm of self-improvement that you lose sight of what is, of who you are right now, and what is great about this version of you. The truth is that you are worthy of love now. You are already making an effort to be a good person and fulfill your duties. This isn't to say you can't benefit from change or further honing your skills—after all, life is a work in progress—but it's important to focus first on loving yourself as you are right now; otherwise, you can end up in a never-ending race for more. In fact, true self-love *begins* when you set aside "I could" and "I should" in favor of "I am."

TAKING ACTION

Do you beat yourself up for not reaching some imaginary standard? Maybe you want to be thinner or richer or more successful. Take the hurting part of yourself you've been focusing on and say to yourself, "It's okay. I love you for who you are. You can stop struggling. I love you no matter what." Repeat this phrase until you start to truly feel it in your heart.

Curb Vision Waterboarding

Finding fault and feeling hopeless about improving the situation produces resignation....Blindly believing that everything will work out just fine also produces resignation, for we have no motive to apply ourselves toward making things better. But in order to survive—both as individuals and as a civilization—and especially in order to thrive, we need the right balance of critical thinking and hope.

—Maria Popova, writer

Have you ever made a vision board? You wanted something to happen in your life—like finding your true love, buying your dream house, or landing your ideal job—so you took some poster board, a stack of magazines, and an economy-sized pack of glue sticks and made the most perfect collage of your dreams. You made sure to do the affirmations and visualizations, you worked on your goals, and you gave your dream a deadline, but it just didn't happen. Maybe you didn't create a physical vision board, but you held that picture of success in your mind and worked hard at it. Still, it didn't turn out as you'd hoped. You may have then entered the stage known as "vision waterboarding," where you torture yourself to discern what you might have done wrong or where you could have tried something different to make your dream a reality. Amazing things can happen through the power of the mind, but it shouldn't be a torturous procedure that keeps you from loving what is. Sometimes life gets in the way, your priorities and/or circumstances change, or events intercede. The fact that your vision has not (yet) come true doesn't mean there's something wrong with you. Give yourself the grace to let it go, do something else, dream a new dream.

TAKING ACTION

Have you ever fixated on a vision? The tendency to desire and expect a certain outcome may sometimes be adaptive, as it can lead to dogged determination, but it can also be devastating when the expected vision doesn't materialize. What visions for your future do you have right now? What will you do if your plan comes together? What will you do if it doesn't? Consider how you would process the possible outcomes.

Break Through the Cocoon

You have the power to create even more magic in your life through simple, everyday actions; and the Universe always rewards action....You'll be rewarded in thousands of small ways that make it worth it. But you have to start before you're ready. Show the Universe that you're worth it now.

—Denise Duffield-Thomas, author of *Get Rich, Lucky Bitch!: Release Your Money Blocks and Live a First-Class Life*

You may sometimes focus so much on what could go wrong that you forget to think about what could go *right*. This is where the ego comes in. The ego wants you to stay protected and safe, to create a cocoon around you that bad things can't break through, but at some point that cocoon has to break open and fall to the ground so you can live life to the fullest. Everyone makes mistakes. There will be plans that don't come to fruition and a whole lot of mishaps and missteps. None of this means your life isn't going well. Every so-called failure is a learning opportunity. While we would all like a straight line from point A to point B, from the life we have now to the life of our dreams, everyone struggles at some point. Just remember that not *everything* will be a struggle when you take the chance to live outside the cocoon. There will be moments of immense satisfaction and exhilaration, times when plans come together, even if it's in ways you didn't expect. The good times are enabled by the time spent slogging away. Struggle and reward are two sides of the same coin.

TAKING ACTION

Have you been refraining from some action because you're worried about things going wrong? Give yourself permission to take a small step forward in life, even if it flops. This could be anything from asking someone out on a date to taking a guitar class to repainting your living room.

Tend to Your Duties

Realize that you must go forward at a beginner's pace. Take baby steps. Be proud of each faltering toddle, each newly taken footstep. Become a kind and encouraging parent to yourself. Gently congratulate yourself on your successes and comfort yourself after failure.

—Sue Patton Thoele, psychotherapist and author of *The Courage to Be Yourself: A Woman's Guide to Emotional Strength and Self-Esteem*

It can be easy to get lost in planning, forgetting that life operates on its own timetable. The truth is that life doesn't require any forecasting ability. You only have to be present in your life as it unfolds, to simply show up—for your family, your job, and yourself. If you attend to your duties daily, you will have done your part, and no one can ask any more of you than that. In this chaotic and unpredictable world, an adherence to duty provides a reliable guide to help you stay the course. If you mind your duties to others and yourself, you can find a place of rest in the midst of activity and go confidently into the future knowing what you must do. You may not always know what will happen but you do know where your responsibilities lie. Fulfilling your duties is a simple way to act out of love for yourself and your life. When you perform your duties, you put in the effort needed to live happily and prosperously and you can lay down the belief that you are responsible for anything else.

TAKING ACTION
Make some lists of the duties in your life. This is not a to-do list, more like a job description for each part of your life. In what areas might you be falling behind or going ahead of your duty? Think about how you might bring things into line with consistent attention and effort. You'll know when you have it right when you feel neither exhausted nor under-involved.

Nurture Your Relationships

Since there is no separation between lover and beloved, self-love truly reaches to the deepest interior or heart of the person....The interior life and self-experience of each person constituted by self-love and actualized in self-friendship, in turn, creates the terms for friendship between persons.

—Anthony T. Flood, author of *The Root of Friendship: Self-Love and Self-Governance in Aquinas*

As in many languages around the world, English uses three "persons": first (I, we), second (you), and third (he, she, they). This division really amounts to a sort of quirk in language as there is a good bit of we in I and a good bit of I in you. After all, people are social animals through and through. Every time we say I, the other two persons are often there as well, implied behind the scenes. For example, you may go to the store to buy food for your whole family or you want to do well in your career to provide for your dependents. To manifest self-love, you have to work on all your relationships and speak in all three persons. As you nurture your bonds with the important people in your life, you feed the social animal within yourself. You feel more and more satisfaction and joy each day as you connect on deeper levels with those who bring out your best self—those who show you just how worthy of love you truly are. The good thing is you don't have to be perfect; you just have to be patient and understanding, to simply try—both with yourself and your loved ones.

TAKING ACTION

What are some things you do for yourself that may also benefit the other people in your life? For example, you may take care of your health so you can have a longer retirement with your spouse in old age. Make a list of three to five things that benefit you as well as others. Keep your list where you can see it regularly as a reminder that you are not alone in this life: You are needed by—and need—others.

A healthy self-love means
we have no compulsion to justify
to ourselves or others why we take
vacations, why we sleep late, why we
buy new shoes, why we spoil ourselves
from time to time. We feel comfortable
doing things which add quality
and beauty to life.

—Andrew Matthews, author

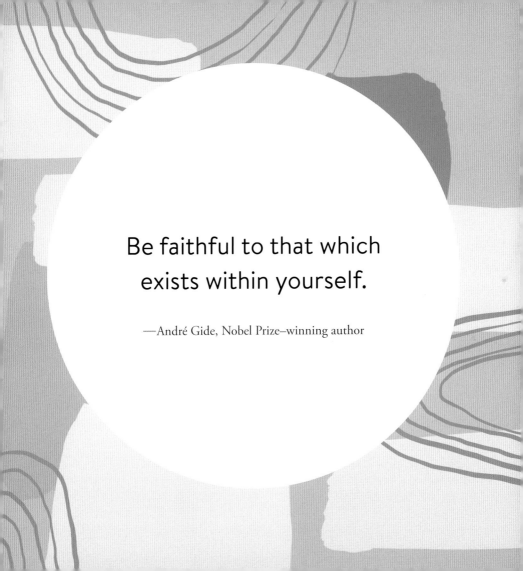

Be faithful to that which
exists within yourself.

—André Gide, Nobel Prize–winning author

Work with Heart

The cult of numbers that masquerades as rationalization has momentous consequences: it changes the way we construct and understand value or desirability.

—Steffen Mau, author of *The Metric Society: On the Quantification of the Social*

People tend to judge themselves in terms of productivity—by the number of items checked off their to-do lists, the number of end products they've generated, or the number of interactions with clients or customers. For that matter, many use apps that track numbers: number of steps taken, number of calories consumed, or number of minutes meditated. You can focus so much on quantity that you forget about quality: how graceful you were during a challenge, how kind you were to a coworker during a project, how satisfied you feel after a job well done. And that's what matters! Your heart doesn't really care how much work is completed. It cares about those intangible qualities like kindness, patience, and contentment, about your value as a person, not as a producer, and it cares about other people in the same way. When you develop a focus around what your heart cares about, you find yourself living by a different set of values, with an indifference to worldly success and a desire for what makes you feel loved and at peace. There is nothing wrong with wanting to be successful in a career or effective as an employee, but in order to love yourself properly, you should no longer take quantitative measures as the sole indicators of your worth.

TAKING ACTION

Set aside your to-do list for today and focus on a quality you'd like to practice. Choose one value word like *peace*, *kindness*, *clarity*, or *imagination* and try to live that value throughout the day in every decision and action. Try to infuse all your working, thinking, and feeling with that quality. If you get distracted, gently refocus by repeating your value word.

Be a Little Silly

If employees are often working through lunch, it's either because they feel they don't have time to stop working, or they believe management doesn't condone taking breaks....Expecting that employees will perform well while working eight hours nonstop is ridiculous. Moreover, it signals to them that leadership only values their work output, not their contribution to the culture or personal commitment to the organization.

—Kate Heinz, business writer

With modern technologies, you can work from anywhere: sitting on the beach with an iced tea or in your living room wearing pajamas. You can be just as effective in a T-shirt and jeans as you can in a suit. So why do businesses still insist on offices and cubicles, business casual or business dress? It may come down to the idea of the "serious person," the person who "gets things done." The serious person works twelve-hour days and takes a twelve-minute lunch while sitting at their desk. The serious person wears dry-clean-only clothes and listens to business audiobooks on their way to work. The serious person responds to every email within minutes and prepares a thirty-page report over the weekend. It may seem like dedication and success on paper, but living this way can take a huge toll on your emotional and physical health. You need to be able to go home and not think about work all the time, to enjoy your hobbies and activities with family and friends. You need to not be on call 24/7. Sometimes you need to take a long lunch, make pancakes on a Saturday morning, or lie in a hammock on a Sunday afternoon. You need your evenings and weekends. In short, you need to be a real human being and not a serious person. Acting out of love for yourself means nourishing all areas of your life, not just your professional life, and happiness comes from fun just as much as it does success.

TAKING ACTION

Do you have in your mind an idea of what it means to be a serious person? Is this stereotype helping you find a good work-life balance or is it hindering you? Name some things you can do this week to maintain a healthy perspective on work so it remains fulfilling without demanding too much of you.

Interrupt Critical Thoughts

Most of the time, when we're being too hard on ourselves, we do it because we're driven by a desire to excel and do everything right, all the time. This entails a lot of self-criticism, and that persecutory inner voice that constantly tells us how we could've done things better is a hallmark of perfectionism.

—Ana Sandoiu, medical writer

For many, self-criticism can feel as natural as breathing. You may criticize aspects of your embodiment, like your weight, skin, or hair; your work habits, relationship choices, or creative decisions; or a financial mistake, like not saving enough or taking on too much debt. This process of self-criticism, of constant and unrelenting negative attacks, directs vast amounts of energy toward self-defeating behavior. You may spend so much time criticizing that you end up feeling uncertain of how to proceed in any ambition. Maybe you give up trying altogether, or perhaps your inner critic takes away your ability to feel proud of a job well done because it always points out what could be better. You likely treat yourself worse than you'd treat an enemy, saying things to yourself you would never say out loud to someone else. Putting an end to self-criticism is a long process that doesn't occur overnight. For some, it can even be a lifelong undertaking. Rather than attempting to take on this immense challenge from the start—or deem it hopeless—you can choose an easier path to victory over self-criticism: Interrupt the thoughts with something positive. Your inner critic has a far more difficult time speaking when another voice, one of encouragement and optimism, is talking. It may even forget what it was trying to say in the first place.

TAKING ACTION

Today, implement a process of interrupting self-criticism. Begin by noticing a negative thought you have about yourself, then insert a pause in this self-criticism. Finally, interrupt the negativity with something positive, such as "These earrings look really nice on me." Keep repeating this process through-out the day.

Align with the Universe

When one's self arises all arises;
when one's self becomes calm all becomes calm.

To the extent we behave with humility,
to that extent good will result.

If the mind becomes still,
one may live anywhere.

—Sri Ramana Maharshi, Hindu sage

One of the oldest teachings in self-love centers around the deep connection between individuals and the natural world. The universe is not just all around you but also in the energies that flow through you, from your mind to your heart to the feet that ground you. It also connects you to all the life around you. It's all too easy to overlook these connections and energies, to feel as if you're alone in your struggles and to resist the changes and detours the universe sends your way. Survival instinct says you must fight, but when you work against the general flow of things, you actually prevent your own joy, your own deeper love for yourself. You block the energy centers (known in Eastern tradition as chakras) that fuel insight and intuition, confidence and focus, self-expression and creativity, love and inner peace. When you understand this, you begin to realize the world is not an enemy trying to foil your plans and create obstacles to your happiness but your partner. It can help you cultivate a foundation of self-love to weather any storm, but you have to cooperate in the process, which you can do simply by being open to the world's guidance.

TAKING ACTION

Today, keep your thoughts and feelings close to home. Each time something arises in your mind, inquire into it. Ask, "Where does this thought come from? To whom is it addressed?" Trace thoughts back to their source and challenge their intentions. What thoughts may be pushing you to close your mind or your heart? What thoughts may be pushing you to open up further?

Let Go of Control

A smile because the nights are short!
And every morning brings such pleasure
Of sweet love-making, harmless sport:
Love that makes and finds its treasure;
Love, treasure without measure.

—Christina Rossetti, author of "A Smile and a
Sigh," from *Complete Poems and Stories*

Life brings a never-ending stream of good things, including pleasant physical sensations, and none of these earthly delights should be viewed as wrong in and of themselves. People go wrong only when they want to control the flow of pleasant sensations, when they want to possess them and hold on to them. If you say to yourself, "I want this and I want it now," you suffer. After all, you can control what you think and do but you cannot control the results that come your way (as much as we may wish that weren't true). If you instead say, "I am willing to accept whatever life brings," you find peace. You appreciate what good things come without trying to control them (to no avail). Practicing self-discipline in your desires will keep you from frustration or self-blame when something good passes. This path leads not only to contentment but also to bliss, because this is an abundant world with plenty of good things for everyone. The mistake lies in not noticing the good things here at hand. When you recognize the good things in your own life and feel thankful for them as they are, you build a love that radiates from what you have to who you are.

TAKING ACTION

When a complaint comes into your mind, redirect it. You can try concentrating your mind on being grateful for something good that's already come into your life or thinking of a few action items that address your particular complaint. For example, if you don't have enough money to pay your electric bill, you might call your utility company to ask for an extension. Keep practicing these redirection strategies throughout the day.

Read Beyond the Label

*Acceptance is an immediate consent to something
which is judged to be good, and self-love is in
essence an acceptance of this kind....It is an abiding
attitude which might be expressed in words like
these: "I'm here! And I'm like this! Hurray!"*

—John Cowburn, philosopher

Two of the most common labels you may hear in daily life are introvert and extrovert. These labels refer to how people relate to themselves and the world around them. An introvert typically spends more time exploring their own thoughts and feelings and may require alone time to recharge. An extrovert spends more time focused on what exists outside their own mind and enjoys quality time with others to recharge. While there are benefits to these labels, such as better understanding where you draw energy from versus what may deplete it, they can also be self-limiting. Someone who's an introvert may benefit from pushing themselves at times to make more connections with others, while someone who's an extrovert may consider finding more peace in solitude. There are also stereotypes tied to these labels; introverts are sneaky or shy, and extroverts are egotistical or shallow. Of course, nothing in nature ever falls into a tidy category. Everyone has a mix of tendencies depending on the situation and these can change over time and experience. To love yourself, you cannot let a label define who you are. Surprises come when you stop doing the things you've always done and take a chance on something outside the boundaries of any label you might have for yourself. At the same time, you have to love yourself where you are, as you are, in all situations, and no matter how others might judge you based on a label.

TAKING ACTION

Today, try stepping outside your ordinary routine. Read a book in a genre you wouldn't ordinarily like. Press the "random article" button on *Wikipedia*. Make a weird avatar for social media. Talk to someone who has different political or religious beliefs. Buy an outfit you wouldn't ordinarily wear.

Care for Someone Else

Caring about others, running the risk of feeling, and leaving an impact on people, brings happiness.

—Harold Kushner, rabbi and author

Caring for others does not stand apart from your relationship with yourself. When you take care of someone else, whether a parent, child, partner, pet, or even a plant, you open a space of caring in yourself. This space of caring or caring attitude then begins to pervade your entire life and you start to do everything with greater intentionality. When you bring order into your life, when you cultivate a good environment in your home for someone or something else, you experience the benefit of sane and nurturing surroundings. As you create inviting spaces for others, you're encouraged to do the same for yourself. You can begin your journey toward self-love by taking care of the people, plants, animals, and spaces where you spend most of your time. The effort and energy of care will come across in all your interactions. And remember that caring is not an either/or proposition (either you care for others or you care for yourself). You begin to heal when you care for both yourself *and* the important people and things in your life.

TAKING ACTION

You may have some caring relationships in your life that are mostly one-way, such as caring for an elder or a child who is not able to provide for themselves. Reflect on what joy you take from these experiences of caring and consider what insights into self-care they might offer. For example, a family pet is the perfect reminder to take a break from work and have some fun once in a while. A funny comment by a child may be just what you needed to not only lift your spirits but also set an intention to take things a little less seriously moving forward.

Create a Hopeful Expectation

They say a person needs just three things to be truly happy in this world: someone to love, something to do, and something to hope for.

—Tom Bodett, author and radio personality

As you continue along your journey in self-love, it will be important to intentionally maintain a belief that each day will bring new ways to walk in love, that you will receive the teachings, material things, and love and affection from others that you need all at the right time. This sense of hopeful expectation, this glimmer held in your heart, will be your anchor in self-love when the path feels challenging and you may otherwise be tempted to give up. When self-doubt creeps in, your hopeful expectation will be a shield that drives those negative thoughts back into hiding. Hopeful expectation is the opposite of the self-pitying state of mind many people build up over years of struggling with self-esteem and self-love. Self-pity masquerades as care for your well-being but really amounts to a form of self-destructiveness as you become caught up in negativity and allow yourself to wallow in it rather than put in the effort to change things. Let hopeful expectation be an ally in your self-love journey.

TAKING ACTION

As you go through your day, say to yourself, "Today good things will come to me." Repeat this phrase as often as you can. Continue into the evening and while getting ready for bed. Concentrate on really believing this phrase and noticing when it comes true. Don't let a single good thing go by without inner thankfulness, no matter how small it might be.

Leave No Time for Doubt

Oftentimes, our biggest hurdle to getting what we want and achieving a breakthrough is comfort and convenience. As humans, we are creatures of habit and our brain likes to keep us safe from all types of risk.

—Julian Hayes II, author and health and wellness consultant

Your satisfaction with life and sense of love for yourself improve when you see what you want and take it. Act before your mind has time to waver, before self-doubt begins to rear its ugly head. Take something for yourself, whether a job, material thing, or whatever else doesn't make you a selfish or bad person. You deserve the best that life has to offer. The first obstacle to getting what you want is the self-doubt that questions whether you are worthy and suggests that you are faulty, immoral, or deficient in some way. As a result of doubt, you let things that might change or heighten your life pass you by. You must practice leaving less time and space for doubt by acting on your heart's desires as they come.

When you begin to take the things you want for yourself, you begin to believe in yourself more and more and you find it easier to build more abundance for yourself in all areas of life. Life turns into a good dream where you're surrounded by pleasant people and circumstances.

TAKING ACTION

What can you claim for yourself today? Can you clear a corner of your home to use for your hobby? Can you buy yourself a piece of jewelry? Can you apply for a grant or sign up for a contest? You don't have to claim something big but try to spend some time or money on yourself today. Don't think. Do!

Claim Your Own Well-Being

Wellness culture is thin, white, able-bodied, and largely performance based (can you move in x-amount of ways and contour your body into pretzels, etc.). Our work centers around the idea that it is okay to be wherever you are. That all bodies are different and good. That we make a home of ourselves when we find self-love without trying to be something other, different.

—Caitlin Metz, cocreator of *On Being in Your Body*

Well-being in life does not belong to a select few. It is also not one-size-fits-all. Each and every person has different abilities and resources, but they also have a point of optimal functioning that is unique for them. This point of functioning also changes with each stage of life. If you stop judging yourself by normative measures of success, you can find the state of excellence that is unique to you at this point in your life. You can find what wellness means for you in your current circumstances. You can stop comparing yourself to the images in fitness magazines and work with the body you have. You can feel fit, healthy, and sexy in your own body and truly love and appreciate it for what it does each day to carry and support you in your pursuits. This love begins with a healthy sense of being grounded in reality and accepting your present state of ability and need.

TAKING ACTION

Have you ever gotten an overuse injury because you were trying to imitate what someone else was doing or by pushing too far beyond your skill level? Think about this experience and what you can learn from what happened. Write down a few wellness goals that are realistic for you at this point in your life. (Define realistic as something you can achieve within the next four to eight weeks.) Be specific and give yourself a game plan for how you can achieve your goals, then add this plan to your calendar.

Find Your Purpose

Part of being a revolutionary is creating a vision that is more humane. That is more fun, too. That is more loving. It's really working to create something beautiful.

—Assata Shakur, Black Panther activist

Your work, your speech, your spirit—everything becomes more animated and inspired when you're acting out of a sense of purpose. When you've lost your sense of purpose—the feeling that what you do makes a difference in the world—it can be hard to feel deserving of happiness or love. As human beings, we want to survive, but it's also in our nature to want more than that. We want to live for some reason that feels bigger than just existing from one day to the next, whether that might be building a better sense of community in your neighborhood, rectifying an injustice, or helping in animal rescue. We feel happier and more fulfilled with ourselves and what we've done when we make the effort to bring our lives into alignment with that purpose. If you're unsure of your own purpose or feel that it's slipped out of focus, take a break for deep reflection to find your way back to the reason that drew you to your work, relationships, and hobbies in the first place. Simply taking the first step in exploring what gives your life meaning is an act of love toward yourself. You deserve more than mere survival. You deserve to thrive.

TAKING ACTION

Have you ever had a sense of calling in life? Maybe you had some sort of profound epiphany or maybe you just found satisfaction in your work. When do you feel most connected to your work? When do you most feel like you're on the right trajectory in life? Name a few small changes you can make to bring your life back toward your sense of purpose.

Take Care of the Little Things

Living a meaningful and purposeful life in accordance with one's potential implies having love for the being of one's self and others. Self-love, when authentic, indicates empathetic understanding, awareness, compassion, devotion, generosity, kindness, honor, and acceptance of one's self and others.

—Sepideh Irvani, psychologist and author of *Authentic Self-Love: A Path to Healing the Self and Relationships*

Many people abandon self-love and self-care when they most need good, positive lifestyle habits. When difficult times arise, the instinct can be to crumple into a ball on the couch or shut yourself in your bedroom and focus on the negative situation and the bad thoughts that are creeping in as a result. The very habits that might be most useful are the ones you may avoid. No one feels like exercising or meditating in the midst of sadness, and it can be hard to call a friend or seek professional help when you're not feeling well. During these times, smaller doses of self-care can make all the difference. One or two small actions per day, like speaking encouragingly to yourself, will be enough to get you headed back toward positivity and self-love rather than harmful self-talk and self-destructive behavior. Each day presents a new opportunity to start over, a new chance to focus on what makes you worth loving.

TAKING ACTION

Think of one or two small things you can do today to make yourself feel good. Maybe you can take a shower, write in your journal, play your favorite album, or draw a picture that illustrates how you're feeling. Make a few small choices each day that leave you in a better state of mind and body than you were before. Give yourself little assignments for your own healing.

Embrace Your Power

*The thing that happens when people get depressed
is all you do is think about yourself in relation to
the world because you have disassociated from
everything else, and then it starts to destroy your
sense of worth, your sense of identity....Everything's
telling you to stop, but you have to never give up.*

—David Chang, celebrity chef

No one is immune from having low moods—moods that affect not just how you see the world but how you see yourself. For many, these moods can last for days, weeks, or even years. The good news is you can heal yourself by taking constructive action when you do find your mood taking a plunge. Things begin to get better the moment you embrace your own power. All you need is the tiniest fragment of belief that you can love yourself. Sometimes, setting this belief in motion may mean applying a "fake it 'til you make it" mindset. Begin by telling yourself that you believe in yourself and acting as though you believe in yourself. Over time, these words and actions will invite real belief. Even if that belief only lasts for a fraction of a second, even if it's very weak at first, it can move mountains. Belief in yourself as a person who is capable and deserving of love grows over time. You are what you believe yourself to be, even if that belief begins as a guise.

TAKING ACTION

Take a few minutes to generate some power thoughts for yourself. A power thought could be something like "I am alive, well, and in charge of my destiny" or "I am flourishing in every way." Be creative and make your own power thought. Repeat your phrase hundreds if not thousands of times to manifest true belief in your words.

Seek Out Your Hidden Guides

You cannot live alone in this world. The way to enjoy life is to meet people like you, to exchange ideas, to learn from each other.

—Eliud Kipchoge, long-distance runner

The people in your life open portals to the further evolution of your soul, and you should not be deceived by appearances. Each person, no matter their status, wealth, or age, can teach you lessons about how to live with more confidence and self-love. When you close your life to relationships, maybe out of fear or distrust, you deprive yourself of valuable guides who can propel your soul forward on your journey to happiness. The practice of self-love requires intentionally opening yourself up to positive influences and inviting in the guides you need so you have help in reaching your full potential. No one should have to face challenges alone. In your own journey toward greater self-love, be on the lookout for hidden guides who have a lesson to teach or a helping hand to offer.

TAKING ACTION

Heighten your sense of hopeful expectation that guides will come into your life today, perhaps from unexpected quarters. Look for help wherever it may come from, recognizing that a teacher may appear in a humble guise.

Welcome Your Fellow Travelers

Humans, it turns out, aren't so bad after all. Though the dominant narrative of our last few years has been one of anger and divisiveness, most of us actually do want to help each other, educate each other, nurture each other, support each other.

—Chip Giller, founder of *Grist* magazine

You likely hear a lot of bad news every day without even trying. From the TV to the Internet to social media, it can seem like struggle, injustice, and malice are lurking around every corner. Amid this focus on the bad, you may often forget you are also surrounded by good. The heroism of ordinary people shines through in the way they tackle their personal challenges and take care of their families, in the way they perform their jobs and take care of their communities. You have this same heroism within yourself, the ability to hold on to your unique personhood and persevere through difficulty. You also have the ability to look around and find a supportive community in the people all working toward being their best and most confident and loving selves. Your journey of self-love does not belong to you alone. You are not a Sisyphean figure, rolling your boulder up the hill alone. Fellow travelers all around you want to join your mission to find self-esteem. The ups and downs of the journey are far easier to face when you face them together.

TAKING ACTION

Did you ever have a friend or mentor who you thought had it all together, only to find out they had struggles just like you, that they weren't always as self-assured as they seemed? You may be putting a certain pressure on yourself to keep this facade of composure going in your own life, but it only serves to exhaust you even more. Today, try to share one of your struggles with a friend. You may find your problem is not as unique as you thought.

Overcome Overwhelmed

*Don't fear the fear. Instead, see it for what it is.
You're feeling anxious. You just are. No need to berate
yourself for this; it will only make you more anxious.*

—Sarah Wilson, author of *First, We Make the Beast
Beautiful: A New Journey Through Anxiety*

Everyone has experiences with periods of fear and stress. Maybe you've panicked about an upcoming exam in school or realized too late that you didn't file your tax return. Maybe you've had a job that was a particular grind or had to work with difficult people. When faced with these stressors, you may have been tempted to give in to being overwhelmed, to watch the negative thoughts and feelings flood in, overpowering everything else in your mind. The impulse to get overwhelmed (and as a result either freeze up, lash out, or run) is a reactive state ingrained in each of us as a means of survival. Of course, survival instincts are not needed as frequently in the present day and can instead make things more difficult. Fortunately, you can overcome your tendency toward stress and being overwhelmed by first observing the situation as an outsider: Who are the players involved and what are the facts? Looking at things more objectively, rather than through a tangle of emotions, will make it easier to create a plan of action. And planning can be a simple expression of—and bolster for—self-love, as you tackle difficulties (ones you may have thought yourself incapable of handling) in a calm and intentional manner.

TAKING ACTION

Take one problem situation you are currently facing and analyze it completely as if it were happening to someone else. You can take notes on the different elements of the issue to help keep everything clear, then make a list of small and manageable action steps that will address this problem. Complete the first action step today.

Own Your Flaws

Instead of saying, "I'm damaged, I'm broken,
I have trust issues," say, "I'm healing, I'm
rediscovering myself, I'm starting over."

—Horacio Jones, author

For many, a major obstacle to self-love is the belief they are "damaged goods," that they are less than other people due to a certain flaw or past trauma and thus not as deserving of love. At some point in your development, maybe during childhood or your formative young adult years, you may have internalized this message and, once it became lodged there, you found it very difficult to pry loose. Things begin to look better when you understand this truth: There is nothing wrong with you. You are not sinful or incapable. You are unique and powerful. You are worthy of love and respect, of honor and caring. Nothing you have done or will ever do can alter this fact. You need only go and be free. Let your heart well with enthusiasm at this fact. Do you make mistakes sometimes? Yes, but this is beside the point. A flaw in a diamond does not make it any less of a diamond. In fact, the flaw makes the diamond real and legitimate. The same holds true for you.

TAKING ACTION

Go back and read this lesson again. Were there any moments when you found yourself scoffing or disbelieving? Inquire deeply and root out the doubt. Think of this self-doubt as an infection that's overtaken your mind. You may find it helpful to visualize the infection. What does it look like? How is it behaving? Now read the previous paragraph again, deliberately and consciously believing in your own self-worth.

Take Care of Your Needs

Think of a boundary as a healthy space around you. You decide how big this space needs to be for you to feel comfortable. It may be an actual space, measured as physical distance, or an imaginary psychological/emotional space. When you successfully maintain healthy emotional boundaries, you are taking care of yourself first and foremost.

—Abigail Brenner, psychiatrist

You may not really have what you need in your life right now. Maybe you need more free time or more spending money, more affection or more intimacy, a new car or a vacation. Struggles with self-love can often point to these unmet needs. Loving yourself means not denying your needs or trying to go without them but taking action to secure the things you need, whether they are tangible items or intangible values, because you are deserving. This process of fulfilling your needs begins with the mind.

First, form vivid pictures in your head of exactly what you need. Next, ask that action steps be shown to you that lie within your power in the present. Finally, execute these action steps until your needs have been fulfilled. Until that time comes, don't be shy about asking for help in meeting your needs. There's nothing shameful in reaching out to others so you can find the care you need. Once you have all the basics under control, you can begin to work on the little luxuries that make life more enjoyable and that grow your sense of self-worth even more.

TAKING ACTION

Identify an unmet need in your life, then work through the four steps outlined in this exercise: 1. Visualize your need in detail. 2. Ask to be shown action steps you can take right now. 3. Take the first step toward fulfilling your need. 4. Ask for help if you need it.

Until you value yourself,
you won't value your time.
Until you value your time,
you will not do anything with it.

—M. Scott Peck, psychiatrist and author of
*The Road Less Traveled: A New Psychology of Love,
Traditional Values, and Spiritual Growth*

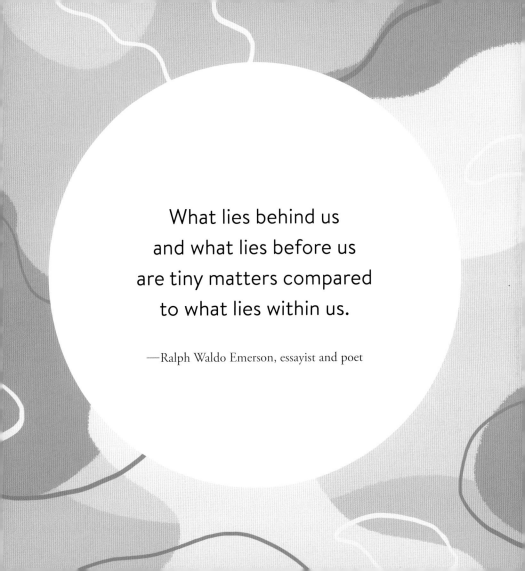

What lies behind us
and what lies before us
are tiny matters compared
to what lies within us.

—Ralph Waldo Emerson, essayist and poet

Work with Imperfection

Sometimes life does not go as you want or expect.
You get disappointed and you disappoint others.
You do not know how to handle new experiences and
you get angry and disappointed with yourself.
Each experience you go through and how you respond
adds to your resources and problem-solving skills.
The need to be perfect prevents you from processing
the experience and learning from it by redirecting
your mental resources into self-criticism and regret.

—Katherine Broadway, counselor

We all live and work in less-than-perfect circumstances. Maybe you work with a difficult person (or two), you don't receive payments or materials on time, or you have frequent interruptions. Cars break down, pipes leak, the Wi-Fi goes down. You can handle these situations as they come, but there will always be obstacles. Nothing in life is perfect. Rather than fighting against these imperfections, you have to accept and work *with* them, building them into your designs. As someone who struggles with self-love and self-acceptance, you have already been through difficulty and survived. You may face challenges now—whether new or continued—but they are nothing compared to your awesome ability to adapt and persevere. Tap in to your own creativity and the skills you have built up through your struggles and victories with self-love to overcome and adapt to whatever imperfections life may send your way. See what you can do with a less-than-ideal situation, and you will see part of what makes you worthy of love.

TAKING ACTION

Your struggles with self-love have made you a stronger person, and you hold within you a great ability to heal yourself, even if you don't believe it yet. Take a few minutes to write a mission statement or manifesto for what you think your life up to this point has taught you. How do you think others could learn from what you've experienced?

Recognize Your Inherent Worth

You are your best thing.

—Toni Morrison, Nobel Prize–winning author of *Beloved*

You have been through a lot in life. You may not even share everything you've gone through, perhaps for fear of alienating people, even those closest to you, or because you feel a certain challenge wasn't "big enough" to be worth their time. You may also feel unremarkable from time to time, like you have no special traits or abilities, or you may feel lonely, like no one could possibly understand what you're going through. But despite what self-doubt may be telling you, you are, in fact, a gifted person, someone who will make (and has likely already made) a difference in the lives of others. You are one of those lucky few who has turned a corner, who has recognized a lack of self-love and chosen to change that. Your struggles with self-love are a sign of your humility, empathy, and intelligence. As you work through the lessons and activities in this book, you are beginning to see the fruits of your struggles and triumphs in accepting yourself. You no longer have to put yourself in last place. You matter.

TAKING ACTION

Take the time now to share with one other person something you have learned about self-love. You could post something anonymously on the Internet, share in a conversation with a friend, or post a video on social media.

Step Out of the Shadows

Love consists not only in affections but also in deeds. Love impels us to acts, expresses itself and is proved by acts. Love without acts would not be true and genuine love, which should be not only affective but effective also.

—Fr. Louis Verheylezoon, S.J., priest and author of *Devotion to the Sacred Heart: Objects, Ends, Practice, Motives*

Sometimes we surround ourselves with people who have traits we admire, traits we would like to develop for ourselves. You may feel the need to be more assertive, for example, so you gravitate toward a highly assertive person as a partner, or you may want better fashion sense, so you befriend a coworker who is good with clothes. This is a perfectly normal habit, but a part of practicing self-love means looking to yourself as the source of your own well-being. You realize through these practices you can do things for yourself, buy things for yourself, and experience things for yourself. Before beginning your journey of self-love, and perhaps even during this journey, you may have given others the spotlight. Now you are shifting roles and occupying center stage in your own life. Surrounding yourself with admirable people is still a great thing—you encourage one another in habits and traits that nurture the best versions of yourselves—however, as you grow in self-love, you also recognize what you bring to your relationships. Relationships are a give-and-take centered around mutual respect. No one person should idolize another while ignoring their own strengths.

TAKING ACTION

Think of one priority that you have in your life—something that you want to achieve that is not for someone else. Dedicate one hour today to that vision, side project, or idealistic musing. See how it feels to center yourself in your own story rather than keeping to the sidelines.

Unlock Your Calm Center

The body is not an external instrument which the soul has
happened upon, and consequently uses,
as a musician might happen upon a piano.
The body is the organ of the soul because by the body
the soul expresses and realizes its own nature.
It is the outward form and living manifestation of the soul.

—John Dewey, philosopher, social reformer, and educator

Beneath the fog of the thinking mind and reactive emotions lies the calm center of your being. You can tell you are acting from the center of your being when you no longer hesitate and second-guess yourself. Everything happens effortlessly and easily. Your embodiment, your physical body along with its clothing and adornments, can be put in service of your true self. When this happens, your movements become automatic as the higher consciousness takes over and guides your actions in the right direction. The thinking mind, too, is affected when you act from your center. Thoughts no longer feel labored or tense, the right words come at the right time, and the mind solves problems easily. When everything falls into alignment with your center, you move seamlessly between spirit and flesh and you find no separation between the two. Self-love comes from this complete union of your physical and spiritual natures, when these two aspects no longer war with each other, when you become whole and complete.

TAKING ACTION

You can practice getting in touch with your calm center by doing ordinary things more slowly and intentionally. Take a simple task, like chopping vegetables or going for a walk. Rather than being in charge of what you are doing, allow the movements to flow through you. Surrender control of the actions and simply let them occur. Give up the idea that you are the author or cause of what you do.

Discover Your Style of Life

Take this well to heart:
you must gain control of your habits;
First over stomach, then sleep,
and then luxury, and anger.
What brings you shame, do not
unto others, nor by yourself.
The highest of duties is honor of self.

—Pythagoras, philosopher and mathematician

You may have found yourself sometimes going in circles in life, without a goal or direction. Everyone loses their sense of intention from time to time, and, in these moments, it is important to set aside time for rest and reflection to get back on track. When you have a clearer idea of what kind of life you want and why you want it, your actions will make much more sense and each step along the way will become more meaningful. This greater meaning to every action—every intentional move you make—will in turn manifest feelings of pride and satisfaction that build up your self-esteem with each passing day. You will show yourself how capable you are of carving a successful path. You do not need to have a rigid life plan, and setting deadlines, frankly, often doesn't work, as it turns life into a chore rather than an opportunity. What's more important is to have a "style" of living in mind, as well as some habits you'd like to keep as a part of each day. Maybe you'd like to focus on mindfulness, including meditation, reflective walks, and other practices in your routine that help you stay tuned in to both yourself and the physical reality around you. Or perhaps you want creative chaos: the noisy, colorful, spontaneous non-routine that allows you to paint, sculpt, write, or build whatever you like. You can revise your style of life at any point but it is important to give it some thought now.

TAKING ACTION

Do you know what sort of person you'd like to be? What values are important to you? Make a list of qualities, such as "I want to be creative, kind, smart, and friendly." Put your list on a sticky note and post it where you'll see it regularly, or turn it into a word cloud or design that sparks even more inspiration to live your unique style of life each day.

Make Your Space Your Own

What surrounds us is what is within us.

—T.F. Hodge, author of *From Within I Rise: Spiritual Triumph over Death and Conscious Encounters with "The Divine Presence"*

Your mind doesn't just stay in the gray matter inside your head. You are not *in there*. Awareness or consciousness or whatever you choose to call it roams around. It flies out to meet the world, bounces around the walls, scoots through the zinnia patch, vibrates with music, and shivers with cold. Awareness is a resonance with your surroundings. It is the life of the landscape. Sometimes people say "you are what you eat" or "you are what you think." It would be equally accurate to say "you are the spirit of your place" or "you are what you invite into your life." When you make your surroundings match how you want to feel on the inside—when you bring things into your life that express your vision of what it means to live well and be well—you are actually expressing self-love. You are showing yourself care and respect, taking what you need and desire to be happy into consideration, whether consciously or subconsciously. Bring people into your life who lift you up. Surround yourself with attractive items that remind you of who you want to be and what you value. Strive to make your home look and feel the way you would want your inner world to look and feel.

TAKING ACTION

Can you think of a place that is important to you, a place that feels like home? Maybe you lived there for years or just passed through once and felt at peace. If you can't be there now, can you surround yourself with things that remind you of that place? Find ways to bring that feeling of home into your living areas and workspaces.

Raise Your Standards

If you want to change your life you
have to raise your standards.

—Tony Robbins, life coach and author

A lack of self-love can often lead to low standards for yourself. When you question whether or not you're deserving (or simply feel that you *aren't* deserving), you create a low bar both for what you tolerate and what you desire. Perhaps you allow others to take advantage of you at work or in personal relationships, or you put a lot into your job but never pursue a raise. To improve your sense of self-love, you must set your sights higher. Make your friend group and your dating relationships align with your goals. If someone in your life keeps holding you back, let them go or spend less time with them. Try looking for a new job or a promotion at your current company if you're constantly feeling depleted or your current job description doesn't include a number of the tasks you do during your workday. If you work as a freelancer, consider raising your rates.

Update to "nicer" clothes. Give yourself the constant message that you deserve a higher standard from life. You will likely feel unworthy of this new standard at first, but the more you practice living with the bar raised, the more you will truly feel that it's what you deserve. Self-love will move from practice to deep belief.

TAKING ACTION

In what area of your life do you give yourself less than the best? Do you buy cheap shoes only to have them wear out after a week? Do you fail to maintain your car only to have the problems get worse? Do you let others take credit for your work? Take one area of your life where you experience problems and raise your standards.

Take Time to Daydream

Do not daydream about the problems in your life, the evil in the world, the troubles around the next bend. That is what real life is for. Instead, daydream about things that make you smile. No summer workday is complete without a grown person staring at the wall, just laughing.

—John Methven, author and essayist

Most people don't really believe in daydreaming. They think it's childish and naive. Articles and books written for adult audiences focus on productivity and action as the key to success. It is important to work hard and accomplish things, yes, but without dreams, accomplishments feel hollow. If you build your life around practicality or expediency, you may eventually find yourself feeling tired and uninspired—feelings that wear on your sense of fulfillment. And feeling unfulfilled invites negativity toward yourself, as you wonder about the point of what you do, who you are. Self-love is shadowed in self-doubt.

Allow yourself to sit back comfortably or even lie in bed at least once or twice each week and just let your mind drift as it may. If you get a chance during the day, sit underneath a tree or take a break at your desk and explore whatever comes to mind. You don't need to have a set agenda; simply go into your dream world, complete with imaginary friends and places. Imagine secret worlds that no one else can visit. You may receive advice from spirit beings, or you may imagine your dream house or ideal relationship. These dreams infuse your life with a sense of purpose and they give your mind room to relax. When you give yourself over to daydreams, your mind recharges and you go back to your day feeling positive about what you have to offer the world.

TAKING ACTION

Spend at least twenty minutes today daydreaming. The goal is to follow your mind wherever it leads. If you need help getting started, you might imagine your own getaway to a cabin in the woods or a private island bungalow, your ideal date with a romantic partner, or a conversation with someone you love.

Access the Subconscious

The subconscious mind is the powerful secondary system that runs everything in your life. Learning how to stimulate the communication between the conscious and the subconscious minds is a powerful tool on the way to success, happiness, and riches.

—Gil Mayer, human resources specialist

Your subconscious mind doesn't stop working just because you're not aware of it. Beneath the surface of your awareness, your mind is always working on what matters to you. This is why you often have your best ideas in the morning, like when you're getting out of the shower. Your mind has been working all night while you were asleep, and then that flash of insight comes to you unexpectedly. You may also have this sort of insight while doing something that keeps your hands busy, like driving a car or working out at the gym. Conscious thoughts become instructions for your subconscious mind, and you are always giving assignments to your subconscious, whether you realize it or not. By becoming more aware of what is happening beneath the surface of your mind, you can shepherd it in more loving directions.

TAKING ACTION

Tonight, before you go to bed, give your mind an assignment to work on while you sleep. Phrase it in the form of a command. It could be something like "You will remember the pound cake recipe you forgot" or "You will find a way to make an extra thousand dollars." Repeat the request three times, then forget about it as you do your ordinary ritual to go to sleep. Don't be surprised if you receive an answer sometime the next day.

Invest In Your Future

It seems that the universe paces our empowerment to the speed of our willingness to act on our own empowerment—when the student is willing the teacher appears. But we are required to notice the teacher, the sign, to hear and heed the call or the signal.

—Caroline Myss, author of *Invisible Acts of Power: Personal Choices That Create Miracles*

If you have an area of your life you know will be important to you long term, set up a special savings account just for that purpose. Then, when you have a few thousand dollars saved, convert it over to an investment account, like an IRA or some other investment vehicle (contact your financial advisor). You might want to save and invest for your child's wedding, a dream vacation, a second home, a boat, or an RV. Make sure you choose something that carries a big emotional draw for you so it becomes easier to set money aside. Saving and investing is a simple way to show love for yourself because it demonstrates in a very tangible way that you are willing to look out for your own future. It gives you something to look forward to while also connecting your future to what you do in the here and now. Set up your savings and investments so they are as automated as possible while also making it difficult to withdraw your money easily.

TAKING ACTION

Have you had trouble with money in the past? Take a look at your childhood experiences with money and abundance. See if you can remember some bad lessons around scarcity that you may have learned inadvertently. Challenge yourself to read one financial article, magazine, or book this week.

Make Rejection Your Friend

When you're following your inner voice, doors tend to eventually open for you, even if they mostly slam at first.

—Kelly Cutrone, TV personality and author

Get into the habit of putting yourself into situations where you might be rejected—or, in other words, where you might experience an exciting change in life. If your goal is to have a good romantic relationship, put your profile on a dating app. If you want to be a great writer, send your work to editors. If you desire a new job, send your resume to prospective companies. Practice good follow-through and make sure your information gets to the proper person. It may seem counterintuitive that self-love and rejection should go hand in hand, but they do. To practice self-love means striving to expand your horizons and live the biggest life you possibly can. It's only in living to the fullest that you discover great opportunities, grow as a person, and invite the true happiness you deserve. This entails exposing yourself to rejection, so accept that possibility as a part of self-love. When you get rejected, give yourself a short while to be sad about it, then get up and start all over again. Getting rejected shouldn't be viewed as a sign of failure but as a sign of effort, a sign that you are striving to live your best life.

TAKING ACTION

Expose yourself to rejection at least three times this week. Submit your creative work, apply for a job, or ask someone on a date. You might start a document on your computer or keep a journal to track your progress. Don't judge yourself based on the number of rejections you get but on the number of attempts made. Consider a high number of attempts to be a success, whether or not they led to a yes.

Consider Seeing a Professional

Each and every one of us has our own version
of a disability, something that hinders us....
Do I have a disability? Am I handicapped? Well,
that depends. Are you liberated? I am.

—Daman Wandke, disability advocate and CEO and founder of AbiliTrek

These days, a stigma still surrounds mental health care, such as seeing a psychologist or psychiatrist. Don't let this negative stigma stop you from getting the care you need in order to build love for yourself. Whether you're in a bad state right now or things are actually going pretty well, it can be helpful to have an outside perspective from a supportive professional. Therapy can help you not only survive but thrive. It can be the right ingredient to boost your progress toward self-love and put your life on a strong footing going forward. Even if you don't see drastic changes, you will almost always feel lighter and happier when walking out of your therapist's office. And it doesn't have to be expensive. If you don't have health insurance, there are now low-cost online options, as well as providers who work on a sliding scale. Find someone who works for you at a rate you can afford. You don't have to wait until you have a crisis, so go ahead and call!

TAKING ACTION
What do you associate with psychological and psychiatric professions? Do you think of padded cells in an asylum, or maybe shock therapy and lobotomies? Write down a list of some of these associations, then see if you think they're truly accurate.

Give Yourself the Best Tools

If you are trying to do today's work with yesterday's tools, then it is no wonder you are frustrated and stressed. You can't possibly keep up with your peers that are using the right equipment for the job.

—Frank J. Kenny, author, speaker, consultant, and Institute for Organization Management faculty member

At some point, not having access to the best tools of your trade or hobby will impede your development. If you're trying to learn how to play the guitar, a child-sized plastic model won't cut it. If you're a freelance web designer, you need a nice laptop with the right software. If you're a dancer, you need access to a studio and the right shoes. When you invest in your craft, you invest in yourself. By giving yourself the right tools for your job or passion, you tell yourself that you and your success matter. It isn't materialistic to have the right tools at your disposal for your vocation or pastime. These tools allow you to make beautiful things, put your mind at ease, and do your very best work. Giving yourself the best tools to properly do your job or hobby is a simple way to practice self-love. Put a plan in place to get the tools you need.

TAKING ACTION

Have you ever tried to cut corners by buying an inexpensive or inferior product for your job or favorite hobby? Write about a time when you did this and describe the outcome, then write about how the experience made you feel—both about your work and yourself.

Know When to Make a Change

Coasting keeps you playing small and avoiding the fulfillment of your potential.

—Avery Roth, career change coach

Demoralization, which also goes by the names of burnout and chronic stress, happens when you constantly get negative feedback, plans chronically go awry, or expected help doesn't materialize. Everyone has an off day once in a while, but demoralization has a more pervasive, ongoing nature. It becomes a drain on your sense of self-love, as harmful thoughts creep their way in, questioning whether you are capable or even worthy of what you desire. If you're experiencing this kind of negativity in your work or relationship week in and week out, it may be time to make a change. Some work environments are simply hostile and some relationships are not worth salvaging. If you've given it your best for a long time to your own detriment, it may be time to let it go. If you're unsure what to do, talk with a trusted advisor. Make your life choices carefully, but, at the same time, there's no reason you should remain stuck in a bad situation. You're valuable and deserve the best in life. Sometimes the most loving thing you can do for yourself is cut your losses and leave.

> **TAKING ACTION**
> What are your personal criteria for leaving a bad situation? Make a list of at least three considerations. For example, repeated and failed attempts at improvement, not feeling valued or respected, or having contract terms violated.

Share the Burden

You are not responsible for other people's happiness.

—Unknown

It is perfectly natural for some personalities to click and for others to conflict. Don't make yourself do all the emotional work to make your office, family, or any other group function as it should. Your job is simply to be yourself. You are not an emotional shock absorber. You don't have to be the relationship fixer, the group organizer or task manager, or the one who has it all together. If you're feeling exhausted all the time or like the burden is unfair, it's a pretty good sign that you're taking on too much responsibility for the well-being of the group. You are focusing so much on trying to make others happy, that you are neglecting your own happiness, and ultimately telling yourself that you are less worthy of care and consideration. Having self-love means setting limits and putting yourself first. Let someone else have a turn for a change. Step back and let other leaders emerge, even if a big project falls through the cracks or some big argument occurs. The groups to which you belong, whether an athletic team, your department at work, or your family, need you to be a healthy, happy, and functioning person. By taking care of yourself through this sharing of responsibility, you ensure your participation won't be marred by a sense of unfairness or resentment and you'll be better able to ensure the long-term strength of your bonds. Taking a step back for a while to focus on your own priorities isn't the same thing as being lazy or not caring; it's merely a way to prevent your own burnout and renew your spirit.

TAKING ACTION

Think of all the groups to which you belong (work, side gigs, religious organizations, clubs, political groups, family, friends, sports—as many as you can recall), then think about your role in each of them. Are you the mediator in disputes that arise? Are you the organizer? The go-to person? If you feel fine about your level of participation, you may not need to make any changes. If you're feeling drained, however, see if you can find some ways this week to share the burden with others.

Compete with Yourself

Healthy self-love and self-esteem are based on believing that we have a number of positive qualities and that other people have such qualities too.... Needing other people to be less so that we can be more is a common trait of narcissism, and it's not a very accurate way of perceiving other people.

—Tara Well, psychologist

For many, it can feel automatic to compare yourself to others, at the detriment of your own self-image. Everyone has different skills, interests, career paths, and so on, and when you compete with others you'll always feel as though you don't measure up in some way. Instead, compete with yourself. Try to learn a little more this year than you did last year. Try to increase the quality of your work, just to prove to yourself that you can. Each year, become a bit wiser. Let the little annoyances of life bother you less. Try to be a little happier and friendlier. Be an inspiration to the younger generation and help them as much as you can. In your thoughts, feelings, and actions, make every step align with your highest ideals. If you compete with yourself, you won't have to worry about the competition because you're a person of excellence. When you compete with yourself, you also become a good friend to yourself. Competing with yourself means focusing on constant improvement. When you're constantly improving, you make countless problems in life evaporate; you become your own source of strength and make your own way easier. Loving yourself means wanting to hold nothing back, wanting only the best for yourself in all parts of your life.

TAKING ACTION

Take the time now to set a goal for a personal best: fastest 5K time, most words written in a day, most books read in a week, or any other challenge you like. Now come up with a plan to break your own record in the days or weeks ahead.

Get a Good Night's Rest

*Excessive sleepiness not only affects your physical
health, it has a big impact on your mental health as
well. When you don't get the seven to nine hours of
quality sleep you need, it can heavily influence your
outlook on life, energy level, motivation, and emotions.*

—National Sleep Foundation

The quality of your sleep at night makes a great difference in how you
feel during the day. If you're working on a sleep deficit, it can be hard to
concentrate and come up with good ideas. You may feel sad and irritable,
and poor sleep often leads to a poor diet and overeating. This negativity, and the unhealthy behaviors that stem from it, leave little (if any)
room for self-love, or the positive thoughts and actions that help you feel
more loving toward yourself. Work on establishing good sleep hygiene,
like going to bed around the same time every night and refraining from
electronic devices right before bed. Try not to pull all-nighters and reduce

working late if possible. Taking short naps of twenty to thirty minutes during the day can be helpful but sleeping any longer than that during daylight hours can increase insomnia. You might also want to invest in a good mattress, new pillows, and nice linens. There are also many different apps available to help you get to sleep by using guided meditations or white noise. And if you suffer from a sleep disorder like insomnia or sleep apnea, it's worthwhile to get some medical attention. Deliberately getting a good night's sleep is one of the simplest and most effective ways you can show love for yourself.

TAKING ACTION

You may think bedtimes are for kids, but try establishing a bedtime for yourself this week. Start with going to bed half an hour earlier. Instead of watching TV before bed, try reading a book or listening to music.

Hit the Wall (and Keep Going)

Our greatest glory is not in never falling,
but in rising every time we fall.

—Confucius, philosopher

Just when you think you can't continue any longer with a problem at work or in a personal situation, new resources manifest themselves to help you get through. Marathon runners talk about "hitting the wall" sometime around mile eighteen, when lactic acid buildup in their leg muscles makes them so stiff they can barely move. There is also an emotional aspect to this experience, when it feels like there is no point in continuing and that the whole thing has been a huge mistake. And yet, somehow the marathoner keeps going, putting one foot in front of the other. You have more inner reserves, hidden sources of strength and resolve, than you may think. You only discover what you're truly capable of when you push yourself into situations at the edge of your range of experience. Somewhere near the breaking point lies the potential for personal transformation. Take hold of that potential and realize your own strength by challenging yourself in a way that will require you to get past a certain "breaking point." You can do this—you just need to allow yourself the opportunity. Then, once you have reached the edge, and taken the leap over it, be sure to celebrate. Revel in those loving feelings toward yourself, and remember this triumph when self-doubt tries to sneak into your mind in the future.

TAKING ACTION

You have likely come close to a personal breaking point at some moment or moments in the past. Maybe you still linger on one of these difficult experiences, like the end of a relationship, the death of someone close to you, or legal trouble. If you could reframe this lingering memory as holding the key to a strength or growth opportunity you may have overlooked in focusing on the negative, what message might it be trying to get across to you? As a way of tapping in to this message, replay the event in your mind's eye, then ask for insight related to the experience, for example, "What are you trying to tell me?" After spending some time in silence, see what answers come to you.

You're always with yourself,
so you might as well
enjoy the company.

—Diane von Fürstenberg, fashion designer

I have discovered, just as
my teachers always told me,
that we already have what we need.
The wisdom, the strength, the confidence,
the awakened heart and mind are always
accessible, here, now, always.

—Pema Chödrön, Tibetan Buddhist

Further Reading

Your journey to greater self-love doesn't end with the closing of this book, nor is it the only tool available to you. There are countless resources out there that offer insight into building self-esteem and loving who you are and the life you lead. The following are helpful texts to consider.

Acker, Amy Beth. *The Way of the Peaceful Woman: Awaken the Power of You, Create a Life You Love, and Set Yourself Free*. Clarity Books, 2019.

Anderson, Becca. *Real Life Mindfulness: Meditations for a Calm and Quiet Mind*. Mango Publishing Group, 2018.

Borysenko, Joan. *Minding the Body, Mending the Mind*. Da Capo Press, 2007.

Carroll, Molly. *Trust Within: Letting Intuition Lead*. Grand Harbor Press, 2017.

Goleman, Daniel. *Emotional Intelligence: Why It Can Matter More Than IQ*. Bantam, 1995.

Irvani, Sepideh. *Authentic Self-Love: A Path to Healing the Self and Relationships*. Atlantic Publishing, 2017.

Jinpa, Thupten. *A Fearless Heart: How the Courage to Be Compassionate Can Transform Our Lives.* Avery, 2015.

Myss, Caroline. *Invisible Acts of Power: Personal Choices That Create Miracles.* Free Press, 2004.

Patton Thoele, Sue. *The Courage to Be Yourself: A Woman's Guide to Emotional Strength and Self-Esteem.* Conari Press, 2001.

Seppala, Emma. *The Happiness Track: How to Apply the Science of Happiness to Accelerate Your Success.* HarperCollins, 2016.

Shapiro, Shauna. *Good Morning, I Love You: Mindfulness and Self-Compassion Practices to Rewire Your Brain for Calm, Clarity, and Joy.* Sounds True, 2020.

Siegel, Bernie. *Peace, Love, & Healing: Bodymind Communication & the Path to Self-Healing: An Exploration.* Harper & Row, 1989.

Sincero, Jen. *You Are a Badass: How to Stop Doubting Your Greatness and Start Living an Awesome Life.* Running Press, 2013.

Taylor, Sonya Renee. *The Body Is Not an Apology: The Power of Radical Self-Love.* Berrett-Koehler Publishers, 2018.

Wilson, Sarah. *First, We Make the Beast Beautiful: A New Journey Through Anxiety.* Dey Street Books, 2018.

Index

About the Author

DEVI B. DILLARD-WRIGHT graduated from Emory University in 1999 and went on to receive a master of divinity degree from the Candler School of Theology, also at Emory. She studied philosophy and theology at Drew University in Madison, New Jersey, and eventually wrote a dissertation on French phenomenologist Maurice Merleau-Ponty, which was published as *Ark of the Possible: The Animal World in Merleau-Ponty*. Other publications in academic journals followed, concentrating on philosophy of mind, animal studies, and environmental ethics. One of her academic chapters can be found in *Experiencing Animal Minds: An Anthology of Animal-Human Encounters*, edited by Julie A. Smith and Robert W. Mitchell.

Dr. Dillard-Wright took a turn toward Indian philosophy and religion and began publishing books on meditation, including *The Boundless Life Challenge*, *A Mindful Day*,

A Mindful Morning, *A Mindful Evening*, *Meditation for Multitaskers*, *5-Minute Mindfulness*, and *The Everything® Guide to Meditation for Healthy Living*. She converted to Hinduism and wrote *At Ganapati's Feet: Daily Life with the Elephant-Headed Deity*, which includes some autobiographical material about her spiritual journey. She founded the Anahata Chakra Satsanga (Heart Chakra Society) as an outgrowth of her study of the teachings of Swami Satyananda Saraswati and Shree Maa of Kamakhya, who now run the Devi Mandir in Yuba City, California.

Devi is currently associate professor of philosophy at the University of South Carolina Aiken. She lives in Augusta, Georgia, with her partner, Jessica, and her three children, Atticus, Oscar, and Tallulah.